Lectin-Free
Instant Pot Cookbook

Simple, Quick Lectin-free Recipes for your Instant Pot, Electric Pressure Cooker to Reduce Inflammation, Lose Weight, and Prevent Disease

By Lactin Fred

Table of Contents

Introduction

I wish to personally thank you and congratulate you for purchasing this book: ***Lectin-Free Diet Instant Pot Cookbook – Simple and Quick Lectin-Free Recipes for Your Instant Pot, Electric Pressure Cooker to Reduce Inflammation, Lose Weight, and Prevent Disease***.

The lectin-free diet or the Plant Paradox diet is a diet that eliminates high lectin foods. This diet was founded by Dr. Steven Gundry who suggests that lectins pose a danger to our overall health. Dr. Gundy emphasizes that lectins increase inflammation in the body and causes digestive issues along with other chronic diseases, in addition to weight gain.

The Lectin-Free diet cookbook also features the remarkable instant pot, which is the most globally popular appliance of the modern era. The instant pot serves as a multi-use, programmable appliance that can prepare easy and delicious recipes in a matter of minutes. One of the best features of the instant pot is the ability to perform up to 7 functions all in a single pot, which includes:

1. Rice cooker
2. Steamer
3. Sauté pan
4. Yogurt maker
5. Slow cooker
6. Pressure cooker
7. Warmer pot

With these seven functions, it will save you time, money, and kitchen space. You can cook just about anything in your instant pot, and it will always taste spectacular. No need to whip out your other cooking pots because all you need is one!

After finishing this book, you will find a **14-day Lectin-free diet meal plan**, which will help you kick-start the diet. It is recommended that you use this book daily as it contains a set of healthy, delicious, and a variety of recipes that will satisfy your stomach, make you feel better, reduce the risk of cancer, and avoid gaining weight.

Thank you again for purchasing and reading this book, I hope you will enjoy it!

Chapter 1: Lectin-free diet

In this chapter, you will learn everything about the Lectin-Free Diet, which includes:

- What are Lectins?
- The Bad Effects of Lectins
- What is the Lectin-Free Diet and How Does It Work?
- Benefits of the Lectin-Free Diet
- Risks of the Lectin-Free Diet
- Ways to Reduce Lectins in your Usual Diet
- What to Eat on the Lectin-Free Diet?
- What Not to Eat on the Lectin-Free Diet?
- Lectin-Free Diet Food Substitutions
- Lectin-Free Diet Tips and Tricks

Let's begin!

What are lectins and why they are bad for you

So, what exactly are lectins? Lectins are a special kind of toxic protein you can find in foods such as legumes, grains, seeds, and certain vegetables. You can also find a tiny quantity of lectins in eggs, sour cream, milk, and other dairy products.

You can find lectins in most plants and animals. Lectins are known as an anti-nutrient that can bind carbohydrates together from within the system.

If lectins enter the intestines, it will bind itself to the stomach lining. This will temporarily harden the walls and interfere with your intestines ability to absorb nutrients.

Lectins can be harmful as they could lead to many health problems such as:

- Nutritional deficiencies.
- Digestive problems.
- Leaky gut syndrome.
- Cavities.
- Celiac disease.
- Inflammatory bowel syndrome.
- Increase risk of developing autoimmune diseases.
- Allergic reaction.
- Enhances pancreas growth.
- Destroys digestive enzymes.

In short, lectins heavily found in carbohydrate-rich foods make it tough for our bodies to maintain our cells.

What is lectin-free diet and how does it work?

Lectin-free diet is called many names; low-lectin diet, bulletproof diet, plant paradox diet, and lectin avoidance diet. As the name implies, the diet limits intake of high lectin foods.

Dr. Steven Gundry, who made the diet popular, found lectins are dangerous in the American diet. In his book, *The Plant Paradox Cookbook*, he teaches readers how to limit lectins and opt for healthier choices instead. According to Dr. Gundry, this diet can improve overall health and avoid gaining weight.

Lectin-free diet limits, or avoids entirely, high lectin foods such as carbs, pasta, grains, quinoa, uncooked legumes, unpeeled and unseeded nightshade vegetables, and dairy products. Lectin-free diet promotes healthy whole foods, such as kale, mushrooms, cauliflower, broccoli, asparagus, nuts, and seeds, organic pasture-raised meats, wild-caught fish, and seafood.

Benefits of lectin-free diet

Studies have indicated that following a low-lectin is not only healthy but carries hundreds of health benefits. Some of which include:

- Can reduce belching, intestinal gas, and bloating.
- Helps combat diabetes.
- Reduces inflammation, which in return reduces the risk of cancer, depression, heart attack, stroke, and various cardiovascular diseases.
- Help you avoid highly toxic foods from your diet.
- Brighter and clearer skin.
- Better quality of sleep and increase in energy.
- Encourages consuming fresh vegetables, organic meat.
- Can help you lose weight.

Risks of lectin-free diet

There are several risks involved when adopting the lectin-free diet. Research shows that eliminating lectin-rich foods for an extended period can cause nutritional deficiencies, due to massive amounts of vitamins, minerals, and nutrients that these lectin-rich foods provide such as tomatoes and peppers. Therefore, it is important to make sure you consume a little bit of lectin-rich foods to avoid such risk. Here are some risks that come with the lectin-free diet:

- Whole grains contain plenty of nutrients such as protein, vitamin B, antioxidants, fiber, and minerals; magnesium, zinc, copper, and iron, and these nutrients can help reduce the risk of type 2 diabetes, obesity, some cancers, and heart disease. On a low-lectin diet, you will restrict whole grains from your diet.
- Plenty of vegetables and fruits come with many health benefits, however, on a lectin-free diet, some fruits and vegetables are not allowed in huge quantities.
- Vegetarians and vegans limited in choices, as lectin-free diet reduces consumption of plant-based protein; legumes, beans, nuts, seeds, and whole grains.

- A diet with low dietary fiber can lead to constipation.

Ways to reduce lectins from everyday life

It can be incredibly difficult to eliminate high-lectin foods permanently from your diet. It is recommended that dieters avoid lectin-heavy foods whenever they can – however, that may not be always a choice. Here are ways you can reduce lectins from your diet and occasionally enjoy some lectin-rich foods.

- Use your instant pot! If you are cooking beans, legumes, tomatoes, potatoes, or quinoa, the instant pot is perfect for killing plant lectins. However, avoid using "slow cook" setting as a low-temperature cooking can increase lectin content. In addition, pressure cooking also retains minerals and nutrients from vegetables, making your meals healthier as opposed to other cooking methods.
- When consuming potatoes, bell peppers, jalapenos, apples, pears, or any other lectin-heavy plant foods, peel and de-seed; lectin is heavy in peels and seeds.
- When consuming grains, choose white rice over brown rice, white bread over whole wheat. Contrary to popular belief, under the low-lectin diet, white grains are healthier than brown due to being relatively low in lectins.
- Use olive oil, extra virgin olive oil, coconut oil, and even avocado oil as it can help reduce inflammatory activity and is packed with essential minerals, and vitamins, such as vitamin E, vitamin K, calcium, sodium, potassium, and iron.
- Sprouting your seeds, grains, and beans can help reduce lectin content from foods.
- Fermenting vegetables can also eliminate harmful lectins from foods.
- Don't cut lectins from your diet entirely. Some lectins have desirable health benefits. Reduce lectins in your everyday life so you can still enjoy these foods.

What to eat on lectin-free diet

It is practically effortless to follow a lectin-free diet, as the dietary restrictions are not too constraining.

Below you will find a comprehensive list of delicious lectin-free friendly foods that you can enjoy! Every recipe in this cookbook uses lectin-free ingredients, and once you begin modifying your lifestyle to accommodate this new way of eating you won't dream of returning to your high-lectin ways. Here are food items encouraged for this lifestyle:

Grass-fed meat and pastured poultry:

- Beef
- Ground beef
- Beef liver
- Bottom round roast
- Brisket
- Flank steak

- Short ribs
- Ribeye steak
- Pot roast
- T-bone steak
- Sirloin steak
- Lamb

- Lamb legs
- Ground lamb
- Lamb leg
- Lamb liver
- Loin roast
- Lamb shank
- Lamb shoulder
- Turkey
- Turkey legs
- Sausage
- Bratwursts
- Chicken
- Chorizo
- Salami
- Pepperoni
- Ham
- Bacon
- Chicken drumsticks
- Duck
- Veal
- Goose
- Rabbit
- Quail
- Pheasant
- Deer
- Bison

Vegetables:

- All cruciferous vegetables
- Cucumbers; peeled and de-seeded
- Bell peppers; peeled and de-seeded
- Brussel sprouts
- Broccoli
- Cauliflower
- Bok choy
- Cabbage; napa, chinese, purple, red cabbage, etc.
- Lettuce
- Spinach
- Fennel
- Mustard greens
- Parsley
- Basil
- Seaweed
- Algae
- Sea vegetables
- Mushrooms
- Kale
- Collards
- Watercress
- Arugula
- Swiss chard
- Sauerkraut
- Celery
- Onions
- Leeks
- Chives
- Scallions
- Carrots
- Artichokes
- Beets
- Radishes
- Okra
- Asparagus
- Garlic
- Sweet potatoes; in moderation
- Pumpkin; seeds should be avoided

Nuts and seeds:

- Almonds
- Chestnuts
- Pecans
- Walnuts
- Pine nuts
- Macadamia nuts
- Hemp seeds
- Pecans
- Pistachios

Healthy oils and fats:

- Olive oil
- Avocado oil
- Coconut oil
- Ghee; clarified butter
- Almond butter

Wild-caught fish and seafood:

- Fish fillets; tilapia, salmon, trout, cod, halibut, barramundi, etc.
- Catfish
- Crab
- Lobster
- Shrimp
- Mussels
- Clams
- Scallops
- Oysters
- Eels
- Octopus

Other lectin-free foods:

- Nut flours; coconut, almond, arrowroot powder
- Nut milk, cream; coconut milk, almond milk, coconut cream, etc.
- Cacao powder
- Coconut aminos
- Coffee
- Dates
- Dark chocolate
- Mustard
- Natural sweeteners (Stevia, erythritol, monk fruit, swerve)
- Tahini sauce
- Dairy-free ice cream

What to avoid on lectin-free diet

As the title suggests, the lectin-free diet restricts lectin from your diet. It is vital you avoid lectins for a successful lectin-free diet. The following food items should be avoided:

All grains:

- Wheat
- Flour
- Rice
- Quinoa
- Corn
- Millet
- Cornmeal
- Spelt
- Buckwheat
- Barley
- Oats
- Pasta
- Rye
- Maize

Refined starches:

- White Rice
- Cereals
- All bread
- Potatoes; peeled sweet potatoes and peeled yams are allowed in moderation)
- Cookies
- Flour; nut flours allowed
- Pastries

All legumes:

- Black beans
- Boston beans
- Chickpeas
- Chili beans
- Fava beans
- Green beans
- Green peas
- Kidney beans
- Lentils
- Lima beans
- Mexican black beans
- Mexican red beans
- Peanuts
- Pinto beans
- Red beans
- Soybeans
- White beans
- Pumpkin seeds; flesh and pureed pumpkin allowed
- Cashews
- Peanuts
- Sunflower seeds

All dairy products:

- Milk; whole, powdered, evaporated, chocolate
- Cheese; cheddar, mozzarella, swiss, parmesan, ricotta, cottage
- Yogurt
- Butter
- Soy milk
- Puddings
- Ice milk
- Ice cream
- Buttermilk
- Heavy cream OR whipped cream
- Coffee Creamer

Sugar:

- All sugars
- All maple syrups
- Bee honey, store-bought honey
- Agave and aspartame

Fruits and vegetables:

- Tomatoes; any tomato products, including ketchup
- Zucchini
- Squash
- Potatoes
- Peas
- Eggplants
- Ripe bananas
- Melons
- Goji berries, ground cherries, gooseberries, blueberries
- Tomatillos
- Eggplants
- Bell peppers; if not peeled and de-seeded
- Cucumbers (IF NOT peeled and de-seeded)

Lectin-free diet food substitutions

While it appears that some of your favorite foods are high in lectins, once you learn the healthy substitutions for high-lectin foods, you will be able to still cook and enjoy some of your favorite recipes. Here are some of the best lectin-free diet substitutions:

- Swap peanut butter with: almond butter, walnut butter, hazelnut butter, or pistachio butter.
- Swap wild rice with: cauliflower rice.
- Swap pasta with: spiralized beets, spiralized carrots, spiralized sweet potatoes, spiralized Daikon radishes.
- Swap soy sauce with: coconut aminos.
- Swap wheat flour with: almond flour, hazelnut flour, coconut flour, sesame flour.
- Swap dairy butter with: ghee; also called "clarified butter."
- Swap regular barbeque sauce with: homemade, sugar-free barbecue sauce.
- Swap sugar with: natural sweeteners, such as stevia.
- Swap animals milk with: unsweetened almond milk or unsweetened coconut milk.
- Swap cornstarch with: arrowroot powder or nut flour.

Lectin-free diet tips and tricks

The only rules on the lectin-avoidance diet are to limit the following foods below:

- Nightshade vegetables, such as tomatoes and peppers.
- Acorn squash and butternut squash.
- Starchy potatoes; sweet potatoes are okay.
- In-Season fruits; in moderation.
- Grains, beans, and legumes.
- Cow Dairy.

Avoiding the following food groups can be a struggle. However, with these tips and tricks, you can certainly succeed on this diet.

- Get rid of all high lectin foods in your refrigerator, kitchen, and food pantry to avoid temptations; such as all-purpose flour, sugar, pasta.
- Keep low-lectin snacks available; fresh celery, baby carrots.
- If meals taste bland, enhance meals using sea salt, black pepper, fresh herbs, vinegar, oils, mustard, and fresh spices.
- Don't compromise food quality; diet should be rich in minerals, nutrients, and vitamins.
- Avoid fast foods, deep fried foods, processed meats and fish, frozen meals.
- Find other lectin-free dieters; check out social media; power in numbers, can voice concerns, struggles, questions, accomplishments, ask for advice.
- Experiment with new lectin-free recipes and create some of your own.
- Consult with physician before embarking on lectin free diet; everyone is different and may not be adept at a low-lectin lifestyle.

Keep these tips and tricks in mind and you will be on the path to lectin-free success

Chapter 2: The Instant Pot

The instant pot is the number one selling electric pressure cooker and with plenty of good reason. The instant pot is one of the best multi-cookers on the market, which combines the use of slow cooker, pressure cooker, sauté pan, and rice cooker.

In this chapter, you will learn everything about the instant pot, which includes:

- What is the instant pot and how does it work?
- Which instant pot model is perfect for you?
- Best instant pot accessories
- What do all the instant pot settings and buttons do?
- Best cooking hacks for your instant pot
- Instant pot cooking time chart

Let's begin.

What is the instant pot and how does it work?

The instant pot is a 7-in-1 programmable electric pressure cooker that can perform the duties of a slow cooker, rice cooker, steamer, sauté pan, pressure cooker, yogurt maker, and warmer. The creators of the instant pot designed the pressure cooker to make it much safer than conventional stovetop pressure cookers and other traditional cooking methods.

The instant pot comes with numerous of benefits, such as:

- Vegetables retain their minerals and nutrients.
- Flavors of foods are enhanced.
- Save energy.
- Save space in your kitchen.
- Multi-purpose machine.
- Foods cook up to seventy percent faster.
- Easy to clean.
- Less cooking odors.
- Store leftovers.
- Safe to use.
- Kills micro-organisms lurking in food.

With all the listed benefits, how can you resist the instant pot!

The instant pot is also unbelievably easy to use. The normal procedure is:

1. Add desired ingredients to your instant pot.
2. Close the lid.
3. Seal the valve.
4. Select desired program or press "manual" setting.
5. Set desired time and press start.
6. Once instant pot beeps, naturally release or manually release pressure. Remove lid.
7. You have completed the cooking process. Enjoy the food you made.

But, how does it work? Your instant pot is an electric pressure cooker that runs on the idea of building pressure inside an airtight chamber. As pressure increases in your instant pot, it creates hot steam. The hot steam is then used to cook your food.

Since your food is exposed in a high moisture, high heat environment inside an airtight chamber, this means food will cook at a very rapid pace and leave you with incredibly delicious and moist meals.

Which instant pot is perfect for you?

Every recipe in this book works with any kind of instant pot. However, there are many variations that may serve your needs better than others. Here's a couple tips for finding the perfect instant pot for you:

Instant pot models range in 3-quarts, 6-quarts, and 8-quarts choices. Most people select 6-quart models.

If you are meal prepping, stockpiling meals, or cooking for a crowd, the **Instant Pot DUO80 (8 Quart)** is recommended.

If you are on a tight budget and looking for simplicity, the **Instant Pot Lux** is recommended. The Lux possess 1 pressure cooking option: "High;" which many recipes use in this cookbook use. It also has slow-cook, sauté, steam, and rice functions.

If you love desserts or gentle cooking, the **Instant Pot Duo** is recommended. The Duo possesses high-pressure and low-pressure settings. Perfect for cakes, custards, vegetables, fragile ingredients.

If you are an advanced Instant Pot user or a very precise cook, then you just might want to upgrade to the **Instant Pot Ultra**. This model allows you to customize the settings. Not only does the Ultra offer delay cooking but you can manually set the temperature.

Instant pot accessories

The Instant Pot can cook just about anything you want to perfection. However, to prepare some of those amazing dishes you will require specific helpful accessories. To make your life easier here are some of the most helpful instant pot accessories to have:

- **Glass lid:** Perfect for clear view when cooking, sautéing foods, or slow cooking.
- **Mini mitts:** Ensure safe extraction of dishes from instant pot.
- **Egg rack:** Allows users to make multiple eggs at once.
- **Silicone seal rings:** Prevent odors from previous meal transferring to foods.
- **Steamer basket:** These baskets make your life easier, and dishwasher safe.
- **Insert pot:** Prepare meals quicker and store leftovers in it.
- **Silicone spring form loaf pan:** Use loaf pan to bake cakes, pies, and bread.

Understanding instant pot settings and buttons

The Instant Pot comes with settings and pre-programmed buttons with different cooking times. Following is a breakdown of what each setting and button does:

- **Sauté:** Lightly sear ingredients; onions, garlic, vegetables, meat, simmer liquid, thicken a sauce. Pretty much anything a frying pan would do. To use sauté, remove lid and program temperature to low, high, or normal.
- **Keep Warm/ Cancel:** Turns off instant pot, and warms your food.
- **Manual:** Main button; manual allows you to control pressure level, cooking time.
- **Soup:** Offers high pressure (normal setting); 20 minutes (less setting); 40 minutes (more setting).
- **Meat/Stew:** Set instant pot to 35 minutes at high pressure (normal setting); 20 minutes (less setting); 45 minutes (more setting).
- **Poultry:** Set instant pot to 30 minutes at high pressure (normal setting); 25 minutes (less setting); 40 minutes (more setting).
- **Bean/Chili:** Set instant pot to 30 minutes at high pressure (normal setting); 25 minutes (less setting); 40 minutes (more setting).
- **Rice:** Cooks any kind of rice at low pressure; will adjust cooking time depending on the liquid volume, and kind of rice in pot.
- **Porridge:** Set instant pot to 20 minutes at high pressure (normal setting); 15 minutes (less setting); 30 minutes (more setting).
- **Multi-Grain:** Set instant pot to 40 minutes at high pressure (normal setting); 20 minutes (less setting); 45 minutes (more setting).
- **Slow Cooker:** Control instant pot same way you control a slow cooker.
- **Pressure:** Alternate pressure level between high and low pressure.
- **Yogurt:** Create delicious yogurt; read instructions thoroughly.
- **Timer:** Set desired cooking time by pressing - or + button.

Cooking hacks for instant pot

Hacks to make instant pot cooking more enjoyable:
- Can make homemade vegetable or chicken broths in instant pot and store in refrigerator or freezer for ready-to-use natural flavor addition to any meal.
- Sauté mode to add a nice sear or browning for added flavor.
- Sauté mode to thicken sauces, simmer liquid, without transferring to another pot.
- Always make sure there is enough liquid in instant pot. Many foods require a minimum of ½ a cup of water, stock, or other liquids for even cooking.
- Don't use a microwave to heat food, which dilutes flavor, add food to instant pot, press keep warm or slow cook for delicious leftovers.
- When using frozen meats or frozen vegetables, increase cook time. General rule: double the cook time.
- Quicken slow cooker recipes using instant pot; 8 hours on low setting turns into 30 minutes at high pressure with instant pot.

Instant pot cooking timetable for lectin-free diet

The cooking timetable chart below provides references for specific foods. This is a guide. It is strongly recommended you experiment with your specific instant pot to determine the actual cooking time for ingredients/food. Numerous factors should be considered; such as more or less time regarding thickness of meat, rice types, quantity of ingredients.

General guideline based on the following food groups:

- Legumes, Lentils, Dry Beans
- Meat
- Fish and Seafood
- Rice and Grains
- Vegetables
- Fruit

Cooking Guideline: Legumes, Lentils, Beans

Ingredient	Amount	Time	Pressure
Dried adzuki Beans	1 cup	16 – 20 minutes	HIGH
Soaked adzuki Beans	1 cup	4 – 6 minutes	HIGH
Dried Anasazi Beans	1 cup	20 – 25 minutes	HIGH
Soaked Anasazi Beans	1 cup	5 – 7 minutes	HIGH
Dried black beans	1 cup	20 – 25 minutes	HIGH
Soaked black beans	1 cup	4 – 5 minutes	HIGH
Dried chickpeas	1 cup	35 – 40 minutes	HIGH
Soaked chickpeas	1 cup	10 – 15 minutes	HIGH
Dried cannellini beans	1 cup	30 – 35 minutes	HIGH
Soaked cannellini beans	1 cup	6 – 9 minutes	HIGH
Dried northern beans	1 cup	25 – 30 minutes	HIGH
Soaked northern beans	1 cup	7 – 8 minutes	HIGH
Dried red kidney beans	1 cup	15 – 20 minutes	HIGH
Soaked red kidney beans	1 cup	7 – 8 minutes	HIGH
Dried green lentils	1 cup	8 – 10 minutes	HIGH
Dried brown lentils	1 cup	8 – 10 minutes	HIGH
Red split lentils	1 cup	1 – 2 minutes	HIGH
Yellow split lentils	1 cup	1 – 2 minutes	HIGH
Dried lima beans	1 cup	12 – 15 minutes	HIGH
Soaked lima beans	1 cup	6 – 10 minutes	HIGH
Soaked scarlet runner	1 cup	6 – 8 minutes	HIGH
Dried soybeans	1 cup	35 – 45 minutes	HIGH
Soaked soybeans	1 cup	8 – 10 minutes	HIGH
Dried navy beans	1 cup	15 – 20 minutes	HIGH
Soaked navy beans	1 cup	7 – 8 minutes	HIGH
Dried pinto beans	1 cup	25 – 30 minutes	HIGH

Ingredient	Amount	Time	Pressure
Soaked pinto beans	1 cup	6 – 9 minutes	HIGH
Dried peas	1 cup	16 – 20 minutes	HIGH
Soaked peas	1 cup	10 – 12 minutes	HIGH
Dried scarlet runner	1 cup	20 – 25 minutes	HIGH

Cooking Guideline: Meat

Ingredient	Amount	Time	Pressure
Organic stewing beef	1 pound	20 minutes	HIGH
Organic beef meatballs	1 pound	5 minutes	HIGH
Organic dressed beef	1 pound	20 – 25 minutes	HIGH
Organic beef; pot roast, or steak, or chuck roast, or round, or brisket (dice: small chunks)	1 pound	15 – 20 minutes	HIGH
Organic beef; pot roast, or steak, or chuck roast, or round, or brisket (dice: large chunks)	1 pound	25 – 30 minutes	HIGH
Organic beef ribs	1 pound	20 – 25 minutes	HIGH
Organic beef shanks	1 pound	25 – 30 minutes	HIGH
Beef oxtail	1 pound	40 minutes	HIGH
Boneless, skinless chicken breasts	1 pound	8 minutes	HIGH
Organic whole chicken	1 pound	10 minutes	HIGH
Whole duck	1 pound	10 minutes	HIGH
Ham slices	1 pound	10 minutes	HIGH
Lamb cubes	1 pound	15 minutes	HIGH
Lamb stew meat (large chunks)	1 pound	13 – 15 minutes	HIGH
Organic lamb leg	1 pound	15 minutes	HIGH
Pheasant	1 pound	8 minutes	HIGH
Pork loin roast	1 pound	20 minutes	HIGH
Pork roast	1 pound	15 minutes	HIGH
Pork ribs	1 pound	15 – 20 minutes	HIGH
Boneless, skinless turkey breast	1 pound	7 – 9 minutes	HIGH
Whole turkey breast	1 pound	20 – 25 minutes	HIGH
Turkey drumsticks	1 pound	15 – 20 minutes	HIGH
Veal chops	1 pound	5 – 8 minutes	HIGH
Veal roast	1 pound	12 minutes	HIGH
Whole quail	1 pound	8 minutes	HIGH

Cooking Guideline: Vegetables

Ingredient	Amount	Time	Pressure
Fresh whole trimmed artichokes	1 pound	9 – 11 minutes	HIGH

Ingredient	Amount	Time	Pressure
Frozen whole trimmed artichokes	1 pound	11 – 13 minutes	HIGH
Fresh artichoke hearts	1 pound	4 – 5 minutes	HIGH
Frozen artichoke hearts	1 pound	5 – 6 minutes	HIGH
Fresh asparagus	10 stalks	1 – 2 minutes	HIGH
Frozen asparagus	10 stalks	2 – 3 minutes	HIGH
Fresh green beans	15 stalks	1 – 2 minutes	HIGH
Frozen green beans	15 stalks	2 – 3 minutes	HIGH
Fresh small beetroot	10 pieces	11 – 13 minutes	HIGH
Frozen small beetroot	10 pieces	13 – 15 minutes	HIGH
Fresh large beetroot	10 pieces	20 – 25 minutes	HIGH
Frozen large beetroot	10 pieces	25 – 30 minutes	HIGH
Fresh broccoli florets	1 cup	1 – 2 minutes	HIGH
Frozen broccoli floret	1 cup	2 – 3 minutes	HIGH
Fresh broccoli stalks	1 cup	3 – 4 minutes	HIGH
Frozen broccoli stalks	1 cup	4 – 5 minutes	HIGH
Fresh whole brussel sprouts	10	2 – 3 minutes	HIGH
Frozen whole brussel sprouts	10	3 – 4 minutes	HIGH
Fresh green cabbage	1 cup	2 – 3 minutes	HIGH
Frozen green cabbage	1 cup	3 – 4 minutes	HIGH
Fresh sliced carrots	1 cup	2 – 3 minutes	HIGH
Frozen sliced carrots	1 cup	3 – 4 minutes	HIGH
Fresh whole carrots	10	6 – 8 minutes	HIGH
Frozen whole carrots	10	7 – 9 minutes	HIGH
Fresh cauliflower florets	1 cup	2 – 3 minutes	HIGH
Frozen cauliflower florets	1 cup	3 – 4 minutes	HIGH
Fresh celery chunks	1 cup	2 – 3 minutes	HIGH
Frozen celery chunks	1 cup	3 – 4 minutes	HIGH
Fresh collard greens	1 cup	4 – 5 minutes	HIGH
Frozen collard greens	1 cup	5 – 6 minutes	HIGH
Fresh corn kernels	1 cup	1 – 2 minutes	HIGH
Frozen corn kernels	1 cup	2 – 4 minutes	HIGH
Fresh corn on the cob	2 cobs	3 – 5 minutes	HIGH
Frozen corn on the cob	2 cobs	4 – 6 minutes	HIGH
Fresh eggplant chunks	1 cup	3 – 4 minutes	HIGH
Frozen eggplant chunks	1 cup	3 – 4 minutes	HIGH
Fresh endive	1 cup	1 – 2 minutes	HIGH
Frozen endive	1 cup	2 – 3 minutes	HIGH
Fresh leafy greens; kale, spinach, collard greens	1 cup	1 – 2 minutes	HIGH
Frozen leafy greens; kale, spinach, collard greens	1 cup	2 – 3 minutes	HIGH

Ingredient	Amount	Time	Pressure
Fresh leeks	1 cup	2 – 3 minutes	HIGH
Frozen leeks	1 cup	3 – 4 minutes	HIGH
Fresh mixed vegetables	1 cup	3 – 4 minutes	HIGH
Frozen mixed vegetables	1 cup	4 – 6 minutes	HIGH
Fresh okra	1 cup	2 – 3 minutes	HIGH
Frozen okra	1 cup	3 – 4 minutes	HIGH
Fresh onion slices	1 cup	2 – 3 minutes	HIGH
Frozen onion slices	1 cup	3 – 4 minutes	HIGH
Fresh parsnips chunks	1 cup	3 – 4 minutes	HIGH
Frozen parsnips chunks	1 cup	4 – 5 minutes	HIGH
Fresh green peas	1 cup	1 – 2 minutes	HIGH
Frozen green peas	1 cup	2 – 3 minutes	HIGH
Fresh cubed potatoes	1 cup	3 – 4 minutes	HIGH
Frozen cubed potatoes	1 cup	4 – 5 minutes	HIGH
Fresh small whole potatoes	4	8 – 10 minutes	HIGH
Frozen small whole potatoes	4	12 – 14 minutes	HIGH
Fresh large whole potatoes	4	12 – 15 minutes	HIGH
Frozen large whole potatoes	4	15 – 19 minutes	HIGH
Fresh small pumpkin pieces	1 cup	4 – 5 minutes	HIGH
Frozen small pumpkin pieces	1 cup	6 – 7 minutes	HIGH
Fresh large pumpkin pieces	1 cup	8 – 10 minutes	HIGH
Frozen large pumpkin pieces	1 cup	10 – 14 minutes	HIGH
Fresh acorn slices	1 cup	3 – 4 minutes	HIGH
Frozen acorn slices	1 cup	4 – 6 minutes	HIGH
Fresh butternut squash slices	1 cup	4 – 6 minutes	HIGH
Frozen butternut squash slices	1 cup	6 – 8 minutes	HIGH
Fresh sweet potato cubes	1 cup	2 – 4 minutes	HIGH
Frozen sweet potato cubes	1 cup	4 – 6 minutes	HIGH
Fresh small sweet potato	4	10 – 12 minutes	HIGH
Frozen small sweet potato	4	12 – 14 minutes	HIGH
Fresh large sweet potato	4	12 – 15 minutes	HIGH
Frozen large sweet potato	4	15 – 19 minutes	HIGH
Fresh sweet bell peppers	1 cup	1 – 3 minutes	HIGH
Frozen sweet bell peppers	1 cup	2 – 4 minutes	HIGH
Fresh quartered tomatoes	1 cup	2 – 3 minutes	HIGH
Frozen quartered tomatoes	1 cup	4 – 5 minutes	HIGH

Cooking Guideline: Fruit

Ingredient	Amount	Time	Pressure
Fresh apple slices	1 cup	1 – 2 minutes	HIGH
Dried apple slices	1 cup	2 – 3 minutes	HIGH

Ingredient	Amount	Time	Pressure
Fresh whole apples	2	3 – 4 minutes	HIGH
Dried whole apples	2	4 – 6 minutes	HIGH
Fresh whole apricot	2	2 – 3 minutes	HIGH
Dried whole apricot	2	3 – 4 minutes	HIGH
Fresh peaches	1 cup	2 – 3 minutes	HIGH
Dried peaches	1 cup	4 – 5 minutes	HIGH
Fresh whole pears	2	3 – 4 minutes	HIGH
Dried whole pears	2	4 – 6 minutes	HIGH
Fresh pear slices	1 cup	2 – 3 minutes	HIGH
Dried pear slices	1 cup	4 – 5 minutes	HIGH
Fresh plums	1 cup	2 – 4 minutes	HIGH
Dried plums	1 cup	4 – 5 minutes	HIGH

Cooking Guideline: Fish and Seafood

Ingredient	Amount	Time	Pressure
Fresh crab whole	2	2 – 3 minutes	HIGH
Frozen crab whole	2	4 – 5 minutes	HIGH
Fresh whole fish	2	4 – 5 minutes	HIGH
Frozen whole fish	2	5 – 7 minutes	HIGH
Fresh fish fillet	2	2 – 4 minutes	HIGH
Frozen fish fillet	2	3 – 4 minutes	HIGH
Fresh fish steak	2	3 – 4 minutes	HIGH
Frozen fish steak	2	4 – 6 minutes	HIGH
Fresh lobster	2	2 – 3 minutes	HIGH
Frozen lobster	2	3 – 4 minutes	HIGH
Fresh mussels	1 cup	1 – 2 minutes	HIGH
Frozen mussels	1 cup	2 – 3 minutes	HIGH
Fish stock	1 cup	7 – 8 minutes	HIGH
Fresh shrimp	1 cup	1 – 3 minutes	HIGH
Frozen shrimp	1 cup	2 – 4 minutes	HIGH

Cooking Guideline: Rice and Grains

Ingredient	Amount	Time	Pressure
Pearl barley	1 cup	20 – 22 minutes	HIGH
Barley pot	1 cup	25 – 30 minutes	HIGH
Thick congee	1 cup	15 – 20 minutes	HIGH
Congee thin	1 cup	15 – 20 minutes	HIGH
Couscous	1 cup	2 – 3 minutes	HIGH
Dried corn	1 cup	5 – 6 minutes	HIGH
Whole Kamut	1 cup	10 – 12 minutes	HIGH
Millet	1 cup	10 – 12 minutes	HIGH

Ingredient	Amount	Time	Pressure
Steel-cut oats	1 cup	2 – 3 minutes	HIGH
Thin porridge	1 cup	5 – 7 minutes	HIGH
Basmati rice	1 cup	4 minutes	HIGH
Brown rice	1 cup	20 – 22 minutes	HIGH
Jasmine rice	1 cup	4 minutes	HIGH
White rice	1 cup	4 minutes	HIGH
Wild rice	1 cup	20 – 25 minutes	HIGH
Un-soaked wheat berries	1 cup	25 – 30 minutes	HIGH
Un-soaked spelt berries	1 cup	25 – 30 minutes	HIGH

Chapter 3: Lectin-Free Diet Instant Pot Recipes

Egg and Breakfast Recipes

Broccoli Ham Frittata

Time: 40 minutes
Servings: 4
Ingredients:

- ¼ cup organic ham, cubed
- 2 cups fresh broccoli florets, chopped small pieces
- 4 eggs
- 1 cup unsweetened almond milk or coconut milk
- Pinch of salt, pepper

Instructions:

1. Grease baking pan that will fit inside your Instant Pot with nonstick cooking spray.
2. In a bowl, combine broccoli pieces, cubed ham. Stir.
3. Spread in single layer along bottom of pan.
4. In a bowl, add eggs, milk, salt, pepper. Whisk to combine.
5. Pour over ham and broccoli.
6. Add 2 cups of water, and steamer rack to Instant Pot.
7. Place baking pan on top of steamer rack.
8. Close, seal lid. Press "Manual" button. Cook for 20 minutes on High Pressure.
9. When cooking done, naturally release pressure. Remove lid.
10. Remove pan. Allow to settle 5 minutes before slicing. Serve.

Nutrition information per serving:

- Calories: 423
- Fat: 16.3g
- Carbohydrates: 8.92g
- Dietary Fiber: 1.83g
- Protein: 27.43

Coconut Yogurt with Berries

Time: 1 day

Servings: 32

Ingredients:

- 4 x 8-ounces unsweetened coconut milk = 1 gallon unsweetened coconut milk
- ½ cup of unsweetened Greek yogurt
- 2 Tablespoons of organic vanilla bean pasta
- 2 cups of mixed berries
- 1 cup of Swerve or granulated Erythritol

Instructions:

1. Add coconut milk to Instant Pot. Lock lid, seal lid. Press "Yogurt," adjust to "Boil."
2. When Instant Pot beeps; around 45 minutes, quick release pressure. Remove lid. Allow coconut milk to cool. Stir in Greek yogurt, vanilla bean pasta until combined.
3. Close, seal lid. Press "Yogurt" setting. Set time to 8 hours.
4. Using cheese cloth to strain yogurt into jars. Refrigerate overnight. Clean Instant Pot.
5. Press "Sauté" function on Instant Pot. Simmer berries with granulated Erythritol.
6. Spoon berry mixture over yogurt. Serve.

Nutrition information per serving:

- Calories: 73
- Fat: 6.9g
- Carbohydrates: 10.3g
- Dietary Fiber: 0.9g
- Protein: 1g

Egg Hash

Time: 30 minutes

Servings: 6

Ingredients:

- 12 large eggs, beaten
- 4 medium-sized sweet potatoes, cubed
- 8 bacon slices, chopped
- ¼ cup fresh green onions, diced
- 2 Tablespoons unsweetened coconut milk or unsweetened almond milk
- Pinch of salt, pepper

Instructions:

1. Press "Sauté" on Instant Pot. Add chopped bacon. Cook until brown. Remove cooked bacon. Turn off "Sauté" function.
2. Add cooked bacon to greased spring form pan. Add cubed potatoes on top.
3. In a bowl, add eggs, milk, salt, and pepper. Stir well. Pour egg mixture over ingredients in pan. Cover with foil. Place pan in instant pot.
4. Press "Manual." Cook on HIGH 20 minutes.
5. When done, naturally release pressure, remove lid.
6. Remove pan. Transfer to plates. Garnish with green onions. Serve.

Nutrition information per serving:

- Calories: 394
- Fat: 20.7g
- Carbohydrates: 29.5g
- Dietary Fiber: 4.3g
- Protein: 22.2g

Turkey Sausage Frittata

Time: 28 minutes   Servings: 4

Ingredients:

- 1½ cups ground turkey breakfast sausage
- 1 Tablespoon of olive oil
- 12 large eggs, beaten
- 1 cup of unsweetened coconut milk or unsweetened almond milk
- 1 teaspoon of salt
- 1 teaspoon of freshly cracked black pepper

Instructions:

1. Press "Sauté" function on Instant Pot. Add olive oil.
2. Add breakfast turkey to Instant Pot. Cook until brown, stirring occasionally. Turn off "Sauté" function and set aside.
3. Grease a spring form pan with nonstick cooking spray. Add cooked turkey.
4. In a bowl, add eggs, milk, salt, pepper. Stir until combined. Pour over turkey.
5. Add 2 cups water, and trivet to Instant Pot.
6. Place spring form pan on top of trivet.
7. Lock the lid, seal valve. Press "Manual" button. Cook on HIGH, 7 minutes.
8. When cooking is done, naturally release pressure. Remove the lid.
9. Remove pan. Allow to settle 5 minutes, then slice. Serve.

Nutrition information per serving:

- Calories: 471
- Fat: 31.7g
- Carbohydrates: 4.3g
- Dietary Fiber: 1.3g
- Protein: 42.9g

Cauliflower Pudding

Time: 30 minutes   Servings: 4

Ingredients:

- 1½ cups unsweetened coconut milk or unsweetened almond milk
- 1 cup water
- 1 cup cauliflower rice (pulse florets in food processor until rice-like consistency)
- 2 teaspoons organic ground cinnamon powder
- 1 teaspoon pure vanilla extract
- Pinch of salt

Instructions:

1. Add all ingredients to Instant Pot. Stir until combined.
2. Press "Manual" button. Cook on HIGH 20 minutes.
3. When done, naturally release pressure for 10 minutes, then quick release remaining pressure. Remove lid. Serve.

Nutrition information per serving:

- Calories: 213
- Fat: 21.6g
- Carbohydrates: 6.3g
- Dietary Fiber: 2.5g
- Protein: 2.7g

Sausage and Cauliflower Mash

Time: 12 minutes
Servings: 2
Ingredients:

- 1 large head cauliflower, cut into florets
- 2 Tablespoons of olive oil
- ½ cup unsweetened coconut milk or unsweetened almond milk
- 1 Tablespoon non-dairy butter or ghee, melted
- 1 teaspoon organic mustard powder
- Pinch of sea salt, pepper
- 1 Tablespoon arrowroot powder
- 2 cups ground sausage (mild, spicy – your choice)
- ½ cup vegetable broth
- 1½ cups water

Instructions:

1. Add 1 cup water, and trivet to Instant Pot. Place cauliflower on top of trivet.
2. Lock lid, ensure valve is sealed. Press "Manual" button. Cook on HIGH 4 minutes.
3. When done, quick release pressure, remove the lid. Remove cauliflower, and trivet. Discard water. Transfer cauliflower to oven-proof dish, keep warm at 200°F.
4. In a large bowl, combine cauliflower, milk, ghee, mustard powder, salt, pepper. Use a potato masher to mash the cauliflower until broken apart. Set aside.
5. Press "Sauté" on Instant Pot. Heat olive oil. Brown ground sausage.
6. Add vegetable broth, ½ cup water. Stir.
7. Close, seal lid. Press "Manual" button. Cook on HIGH 8 minutes.
8. When done, quick release pressure, remove lid.
9. Press "Sauté" on Instant Pot. Sprinkle arrowroot flour over ingredients. Allow to thicken, stirring occasionally.
10. Transfer cauliflower rice to serving dish. Spoon sausage, sauce over cauliflower. Serve.

Nutrition information per serving:

- Calories: 618
- Fat: 47.2g
- Carbohydrates: 31.2g
- Dietary Fiber: 11.8g
- Protein: 17.3g

Spinach and Mushroom Frittata

Time: 12 minutes   Servings: 4

Ingredients:

- 1 cup fresh baby spinach
- 8 large eggs
- 6 bacon slices, diced
- Pinch of salt, pepper
- 1 cup water

Instructions:

1. Press "Sauté" on Instant Pot. Add diced bacon. Cook until brown. Set aside. Turn off "Sauté" function.
2. In a large bowl, add eggs, spinach, bacon, salt, pepper. Stir until combined.
3. Grease 4 individual ramekins with nonstick cooking spray. Divide egg mixture evenly between ramekins. Cover with aluminum foil.
4. Add 1 cup water, and trivet to Instant Pot. Place ramekins on top.
5. Lock, seal lid. Press "Manual" button. Cook on HIGH 5 minutes.
6. When done, naturally release pressure 10 minutes, remove lid. Serve.

Nutrition information per serving:

- Calories: 293
- Fat: 20.9g
- Carbohydrates: 3.2g
- Dietary Fiber: 1.3
- Protein: 23.3g

Egg and Asparagus Frittata

Time: 30 minutes   Servings: 4

Ingredients:

- 6 large eggs
- ½ cup of unsweetened almond milk or unsweetened coconut milk
- Pinch of salt, pepper
- 2 Tablespoons fresh chives, chopped
- 1 cup fresh asparagus, stemmed, cut into bite-sized pieces

Instructions:

1. Grease an eight-inch cake pan with non-stick cooking spray.
2. In a bowl, mix together eggs, milk, salt, pepper, chives, asparagus. Stir.
3. Pour mixture in cake pan. Cover with foil.
4. Add 1 cup water, and trivet to Instant Pot.
5. Place cake pan on trivet. Lock, seal lid. Press "Manual." Cook on HIGH 23 minutes.
6. When done, naturally release pressure 10 minutes, then quick release. Remove lid.
7. Remove pan. Allow to set 5 minutes before slicing. Serve.

Nutrition information per serving:

- Calories: 170
- Fat: 13.8g
- Carbohydrates: 3.4g
- Dietary Fiber: 1.4g
- Protein: 9.7g

Chorizo with Sweet Potato Hash

Time: 22 minutes
Servings: 6
Ingredients:

- 6 large sweet potatoes, cut into bite-sized pieces
- 1 pound chorizo sausage, thinly sliced
- 4 bacon slices, chopped
- 1 large yellow or white onion, finely chopped
- 1 Tablespoon olive oil
- 3 Tablespoons fresh rosemary
- 3 Tablespoons fresh basil, finely chopped
- 2 garlic cloves, minced
- Pinch of salt, pepper
- 1 cup homemade low-sodium vegetable broth

Instructions:

1. Press "Sauté" function on Instant Pot. Add olive oil.
2. Once hot, add onions and garlic. Sauté until softened, stirring occasionally.
3. Add chorizo, bacon, and sweet potato cubes to Instant Pot.
4. Pour in vegetable broth to Instant Pot, sprinkle with salt and pepper.
5. Lock, seal lid. Press "Manual." Cook on HIGH 10 minutes.
6. When done, quick release pressure, remove lid.
7. Liquid should evaporated, if not discard.
8. Transfer to serving dish. Garnish fresh basil, fresh rosemary. Serve.

Nutrition information per serving:

- Calories: 590
- Fat: 34.5g
- Carbohydrates: 43.4g
- Dietary Fiber: 6.2g
- Protein: 25.2g

Hard Boiled Egg Loaf

Time: 10 minutes
Servings: 6
Ingredients:

- 12 large eggs
- Pinch of salt, pepper

Instructions:

1. Grease a baking dish that will fit your Instant Pot with non-stick cooking spray.
2. Crack eggs into baking dish. Season with salt, pepper. Don't stir.
3. Add 1 cup water, and steamer rack to Instant Po. Place baking dish on rack.
4. Close, seal lid. Press "Manual" button. Cook on HIGH 5 minutes.
5. When done, naturally release pressure 5 minutes, then quick release remaining pressure. Remove lid. Allow pan to settle 5 minutes.
6. Transfer egg loaf to a cutting board. Slice. Serve.

Nutrition information per serving:

- Calories: 63
- Fat: 4.4g
- Carbohydrates: 0.3g
- Dietary Fiber: 0g
- Protein: 5.5g

Soups and Stews Recipes

Zuppa Toscana

Time: 28 minutes
Servings: 10
Ingredients:

- 2 pounds ground hot Italian sausage
- 1 large yellow onion, finely chopped
- 4 garlic cloves, minced
- 6 cups cauliflower florets, finely chopped
- 6 cups homemade low-sodium chicken broth
- 1 large bunch kale, stemmed and chopped
- 1 teaspoon dried oregano
- 4 bacon slices
- 1½ cups unsweetened coconut cream or non-dairy cream
- Pinch of salt, pepper

Instructions:

1. Press "Sauté" function on Instant Pot. Cook bacon until brown. Set aside.
2. Add ground sausage to Instant Pot. Cook until no longer pink.
3. Add onions, garlic cloves. Sauté a couple minutes.
4. Add cauliflower florets, chicken broth, dried oregano, salt, pepper. Stir.
5. Lock, seal the lid. Press "Manual" button. Cook on HIGH 5 minutes.
6. When done, naturally release pressure 10 minutes. Carefully remove lid.
7. Stir in kale; heat from ingredients should wilt the kale.
8. Stir in coconut cream. Season with salt, pepper. Serve.

Nutrition information per serving:

- Calories: 646
- Fat: 43.26g
- Carbohydrates: 17.69g
- Dietary Fiber: 5.1g
- Protein: 52.24g

Chicken Lime Avocado Soup

Time: 18 minutes
Servings: 4
Ingredients:

- 2 pounds boneless, skinless chicken breasts or chicken thighs
- 3 fresh celery stalks, finely chopped
- 2 medium-sized carrots, finely chopped
- 2 Tablespoons olive oil, avocado oil, or coconut oil
- 1½ cups fresh green onions, finely chopped
- 2 garlic cloves, minced
- 8 cups homemade low-sodium chicken broth
- 1 teaspoon ground cumin
- Pinch of salt, pepper
- Juice and zest from 2 limes
- ½ cup fresh cilantro, finely chopped
- 4 medium-sized avocados, peeled, cored, finely chopped

Instructions:

1. Press "Sauté" function on Instant Pot and add the oil.
2. Once hot, add the chicken. Sear 2 minutes per side until brown.
3. Add garlic, green onions, chicken broth, carrots, celery, lime juice, and lime zest to Instant Pot.
4. Close, seal lid. Press "Manual" button. Cook on HIGH 8 minutes.
5. When cooking is done, naturally release the pressure and carefully remove the lid.
6. Transfer chicken to a cutting board and shred using two forks. Return the shredded chicken to your Instant Pot.
7. Season with cumin, salt, and pepper.
8. Top with fresh cilantro and chopped avocados. Serve.

Nutrition information per serving:

- Calories: 402
- Fat: 22.4g
- Carbohydrates: 16.3g
- Dietary Fiber: 6.83g
- Protein: 33.2g

Spinach Shiitake Mushroom Soup

Time: 15 minutes
Servings: 6
Ingredients:

- 1 pound fresh green asparagus, trimmed and cut into 1-inch pieces
- 2 Tablespoons olive oil or ghee
- 2 cups fresh shiitake mushrooms, thinly sliced
- 4 cups fresh baby spinach, roughly chopped
- 1 yellow onion, finely chopped
- 4 garlic cloves, minced
- 4 cups homemade low-sodium vegetable or chicken broth
- 1 cup unsweetened coconut cream
- 1 bay leaf
- 1 teaspoon dried thyme
- ¼ cup of fresh parsley, finely chopped
- 1 fresh lemon, juice and zest
- Pinch of salt, pepper

Instructions:

1. Press "Sauté" function on Instant Pot and add the oil.
2. Once hot, add onions and garlic. Sauté 1 minute, stirring occasionally.
3. Add asparagus pieces, thinly sliced mushrooms. Sauté 2 to 4 minutes.
4. Stir in vegetable broth, baby spinach, bay leaf, dried thyme, parsley, lemon juice, lemon zest, salt, black pepper.
5. Lock, seal the lid. Press "Manual" button. Cook on HIGH 9 minutes.
6. When done, naturally release pressure. Carefully remove lid. Remove bay leaf.
7. Stir in unsweetened coconut cream. Season. Serve.

Nutrition information per serving:

- Calories: 237
- Fat: 8.53g
- Carbohydrates: 10.75g
- Dietary Fiber: 3.8g
- Protein: 8.54g

Leek and Cauliflower Soup

Time: 19 minutes
Servings: 8
Ingredients:

- 1 large head of cauliflower, chopped into florets
- 1 pound leeks, chopped
- 3 Tablespoons olive oil
- 8 cups homemade organic low-sodium chicken or vegetable broth
- 1 bay leaf
- 4 garlic cloves, minced
- 2 celery stalks, finely chopped
- 2 carrots, chopped
- ½ teaspoon fresh nutmeg
- Pinch of salt, pepper
- ⅓ cup fresh cilantro, finely chopped
- ½ cup unsweetened coconut cream

Instructions:

1. Press "Sauté" function on Instant Pot and add the oil.
2. Once hot, add garlic, celery, carrots, leeks, and cauliflower. Sauté until leeks wilted.
3. Add nutmeg, salt, pepper, and broth to Instant Pot. Stir.
4. Lock, seal the lid. Press "Manual" button. Cook on HIGH 8 minutes.
5. When done, naturally release pressure. Carefully remove lid. Remove bay leaf.
6. Use an immersion blender to pulse ingredients in your Instant Pot until smooth.
7. Stir in unsweetened coconut cream, fresh cilantro. Season. Serve.

Nutrition information per serving:

- Calories: 151
- Fat: 10.63g
- Carbohydrates: 13.75g
- Dietary Fiber: 1.2g
- Protein: 2.69g

Chicken Kale Soup

Time: 35 minutes
Servings: 6
Ingredients:

- 2 pounds boneless, skinless chicken breasts or chicken thighs
- ½ cup olive oil, avocado oil, coconut oil, or ghee
- ¼ cup lemon juice
- 1 teaspoon lemon zest
- 1 yellow onion, finely chopped
- 2 garlic cloves, minced
- 4 cups homemade low-sodium chicken broth
- 1 large bunch of kale, stemmed and roughly chopped
- 2 Tablespoons organic taco seasoning
- 1 teaspoon smoked paprika or regular paprika
- Pinch of salt, pepper
- Fresh green onions, diced

Instructions:

1. Press "Sauté" function on Instant Pot. Add 1 tablespoon olive oil.
2. Once hot, add chicken. Sear 2 minutes per side, until brown.
3. In a blender, add chicken broth, onion, garlic, and remaining olive oil. Blend until smooth. Pour in Instant Pot.
4. Stir in lemon juice, lemon zest, kale, taco seasoning, paprika, salt, and pepper.
5. Lock, seal the lid. Press "Manual" button. Cook on HIGH 10 minutes.
6. When done, naturally release pressure 10 minutes, then quick release pressure.
7. Serve in bowls, garnish with fresh green onion.

Nutrition information per serving:

- Calories: 273
- Fat: 22.32g
- Carbohydrates: 2.4g
- Dietary Fiber: 1.1g
- Protein: 15.3g

Chicken Turmeric Soup

Time: 30 minutes
Servings: 4
Ingredients:

- 1½ pounds boneless, skinless chicken breasts or chicken thighs
- 2 Tablespoons olive oil, coconut oil, or ghee
- 1 yellow onion, finely chopped
- 2 garlic cloves, minced
- 1 cup cauliflower florets
- 1 cup broccoli florets
- 1 cup carrots, finely chopped
- 1 cup celery stalks, finely chopped
- 4 cups organic homemade low-sodium vegetable or bone or chicken broth
- 1 bay leaf
- 1 teaspoon fresh ginger, grated
- 2 cups swiss chard, stemmed and roughly chopped
- ½ cup unsweetened coconut cream
- 3 teaspoons turmeric powder
- 1 teaspoon cumin powder
- Pinch of cayenne pepper, Pinch of salt, pepper
- Fresh cilantro, lemon wedges

Instructions:

1. Press "Sauté" function on Instant Pot. Add olive oil.
2. Once hot, add chicken. Sear 2 minutes per side, until brown. Remove. Set aside.
3. Add onion, ginger, garlic to Instant Pot. Sauté until softened.
4. Add cauliflower, broccoli, carrots, celery. Sauté 1 minute. Return chicken to pot. Add broth, bay leaf, turmeric powder, cumin powder, cayenne pepper, salt, pepper. Stir. Lock, seal lid. Press "Manual" button. Cook on HIGH 8 minutes.
5. When done, naturally release pressure 5 minutes. Remove the lid. Remove bay leaf.
6. Stir in coconut cream, swiss chard; until chard wilts.
7. Ladle soup in bowls. Garnish with fresh cilantro and lemon wedges. Serve.

Nutrition information per serving:

- Calories: 428
- Fat: 42.65g
- Carbohydrates: 11.71
- Dietary Fiber: 3.4g
- Protein: 42.53g

Thai Broccoli and Beef Soup

Time: 20 minutes
Servings: 4
Ingredients:

- 1 pound lean, grass-fed ground beef
- 2 large heads of broccoli, chopped into florets
- 1 cup unsweetened coconut cream
- ⅓ cup fresh cilantro, finely chopped
- 2 Tablespoons organic Thai green curry paste
- 2 Tablespoons olive oil
- 1 medium-sized onion, finely chopped
- 1 2-inch ginger, peeled and minced
- 2 garlic cloves, minced
- 3 Tablespoons low-sodium coconut aminos
- 1 teaspoon organic fish sauce
- 4 cups homemade low-sodium chicken or beef broth
- Pinch of salt, pepper

Instructions:

1. Press the "Sauté" function on your Instant Pot and add olive oil.
2. Once hot, add onions. Sauté 2 to 4 minutes.
3. Add ginger, garlic, green curry paste to Instant Pot. Cook 1 minute.
4. Add ground beef. Cook until no longer pink. Stir in coconut aminos, salt, pepper, and fish sauce. Add broth to Instant Pot.
5. Close, seal the lid. Press "Manual" button. Cook on HIGH 8 minutes.
6. When done, naturally release pressure 5 minutes. Carefully remove lid.
7. Stir in broccoli florets. Allow to heat through for a couple minutes.
8. Stir in coconut cream. Season. Serve in bowls.

Nutrition information per serving:

- Calories: 422
- Fat: 34.33g
- Carbohydrates: 5.6g
- Dietary Fiber: 2.9g
- Protein: 27.35g

Roasted Garlic Soup

Time: 35 minutes
Servings: 6
Ingredients:

- 2 bulbs of garlic; around 20 garlic cloves
- 1 large cauliflower head, finely chopped
- ¼ cup ghee or non-dairy butter
- 3 medium shallots or onions, finely chopped
- 6 cups homemade low-sodium vegetable broth
- Pinch of salt, pepper
- 1 cup unsweetened coconut cream

Instructions:

1. Press "Sauté" function of Instant Pot. Add the ghee.
2. Once hot, add onions and garlic. Sauté 3 to 5 minutes.
3. Add cauliflower, vegetable broth, salt, and black pepper.
4. Close, seal the lid. Press "Manual" button. Cook on HIGH 30 minutes.
5. When done, quick release pressure and carefully remove lid.
6. Use an immersion blender to puree the soup until smooth.
7. Stir in coconut cream. Season. Serve in bowls.

Nutrition information per serving:

- Calories: 156
- Fat: 14.05g
- Carbohydrates: 8.17g
- Dietary Fiber: 2g
- Protein: 2.94g

Hamburger Vegetable Soup

Time: 19 minutes
Servings: 10
Ingredients:

- 1 pound extra lean grass-fed ground beef
- 2 cups fresh green cabbage, shredded
- 2 cups fresh red cabbage, shredded
- 2 Tablespoons olive oil
- 1 medium-sized red onion, finely chopped
- 4 garlic cloves, minced
- 3 fresh celery ribs, finely chopped
- 3 fresh orange carrots, peeled, finely chopped
- 1 large sweet potato, peeled, cubed
- 1 teaspoon cider vinegar
- 1 teaspoon Stevia
- 1 cup pureed pumpkin
- 4 cups homemade low-sodium chicken broth
- Pinch of salt, pepper

Instructions:

1. Press "Sauté" function on Instant Pot. Add the olive oil.
2. Once hot, add onions, garlic. Sauté 2 minutes, until soft.
3. Add ground beef. Cook until no longer pink.
4. Add celery, carrots, and cubed sweet potatoes. Cook for 1 minute.
5. Stir in pureed pumpkin, chicken broth, green cabbage, red cabbage, cider vinegar, Stevia, salt, and black pepper.
6. Lock, seal lid. Press "Manual" button. Cook on HIGH 9 minutes.
7. When done, naturally release pressure 5 minutes, then quick release. Remove lid.
8. Stir the soup. Season. Serve in bowls.

Nutrition information per serving:

- Calories: 132
- Fat: 5.3g
- Carbohydrates: 7.3g
- Dietary Fiber: 3.9g
- Protein: 14.3g

Minestrone Soup with Italian Sausage

Time: 28 minutes
Servings: 8
Ingredients:

- 1 pound ground Hot Italian sausage
- 1 medium-sized yellow onion, finely chopped
- 4 garlic cloves, minced
- 1 medium-sized orange carrot, finely chopped
- 2 Tablespoons olive oil
- 1 cup mushrooms, sliced
- 2 cups fresh broccoli florets
- 2 cups fresh cauliflower florets
- 4 cups baby spinach
- 6 cups homemade organic low-sodium chicken broth
- 2 Tablespoons fresh parsley, finely chopped
- 1 Tablespoon low-sodium coconut aminos
- Pinch of salt, pepper

Instructions:

1. Press "Sauté" function on Instant Pot. Add olive oil. Once hot, add ground sausage. Cook until no longer pink, stirring occasionally.
2. Add onion, garlic, carrots, and mushrooms. Cook 2 to 4 minutes, until softened.
3. Add broccoli, cauliflower, chicken broth to Instant Pot. Stir.
4. Lock, seal the lid. Press "Manual" button. Cook on HIGH 8 minutes.
5. When done, naturally release pressure 5 minutes, then quick release. Remove lid.
6. Stir in coconut aminos, salt, pepper, and baby spinach. Heat until spinach wilted.
7. Serve in bowls.

Nutrition information per serving:

- Calories: 486
- Fat: 51.35g
- Carbohydrates: 12.02g
- Dietary Fiber: 1.2g
- Protein: 26.39g

Chicken Recipes

Italian-Inspired Creamy Chicken

Time: 20 minutes
Servings: 4
Ingredients:

- 4 boneless, skinless chicken thighs
- 1 teaspoon olive oil
- 1 cup homemade low-sodium chicken broth
- ⅓ cup unsweetened coconut cream or unsweetened almond cream
- 1½ Tablespoons arrowroot powder
- 1 Tablespoon organic basil pesto
- 1 Tablespoon organic Italian seasoning
- 2 Tablespoons organic minced garlic
- 1 Tablespoon organic minced onion
- Pinch of salt, pepper
- Fresh parsley

Instructions:

1. Press "Sauté" function on Instant Pot. Add olive oil.
2. Once hot, add onion, garlic. Cook 2 minutes. Add chicken. Cook 2 minutes per side, until golden brown. Season with salt, pepper, Italian seasoning. Stir in broth.
3. Lock, seal the lid. Press "Manual" button. Cook on HIGH 8 minutes.
4. When done, naturally release pressure 5 minutes, then quick release. Remove lid.
5. Press "Sauté" function. Stir in arrowroot powder. Stir to coat ingredients. Whisk in coconut cream, basil pesto. Stir. Allow to simmer until thickens. Season if needed.
6. Serve in bowls. Garnish with fresh parsley.

Nutrition information per serving:

- Calories: 242
- Fat: 15g
- Carbohydrates: 5.3g
- Dietary Fiber: 1.8gg
- Protein: 26g

Lemon Chicken

Time: 19 minutes
Servings: 6
Ingredients:

- 6 boneless, skinless chicken thighs or chicken breasts
- 1 small yellow onion, finely chopped
- 4 garlic cloves, minced
- 2 Tablespoons organic Italian seasoning
- 1 teaspoon organic smoked or regular paprika
- Zest and juice from 1 lemon
- 1 lemon, thinly sliced
- ½ cup homemade low-sodium chicken broth
- 1 Tablespoon fresh parsley, finely chopped
- 3 Tablespoons olive oil
- 2 Tablespoons ghee (clarified butter)
- 1 teaspoon organic garlic powder
- Pinch of salt, pepper

Instructions:

1. In a bowl, combine salt, pepper, garlic powder, paprika, Italian seasoning. Coat chicken on all sides with mixture.
2. Press "Sauté" function on Instant Pot. Add the olive oil.
3. Once hot, cook garlic, onions 2 minutes, stirring occasionally. Add chicken. Sear on all sides. Stir in ghee, lemon juice, lemon zest.
4. Place lemon slices on top of chicken.
5. Lock, seal lid. Press "Manual" button. Cook on HIGH 8 minutes.
6. When done, naturally release pressure 5 minutes, then quick release. Remove lid.
7. Serve on a platter. Garnish with fresh parsley, fresh lemon slices. Serve.

Nutrition information per serving:

- Calories: 380
- Fat: 22.1g
- Carbohydrates: 1.8g
- Dietary Fiber: 0.5g
- Protein: 42.5g

Garlic Drumsticks

Time: 25 minutes
Servings: 6
Ingredients:

- 6 skin-on fresh chicken drumsticks
- 1 teaspoon olive oil
- ¼ cup homemade low-sodium chicken broth
- ½ cup low-sodium coconut aminos
- 2 garlic cloves, minced
- ½ onion, finely chopped
- 1 1-inch fresh ginger, peeled and minced
- 2 Tablespoons cider vinegar
- 2 Tablespoons stevia
- Pinch of salt, pepper

Instructions:

1. Season drumsticks with salt, pepper.
2. Press "Sauté" function on Instant Pot. Add the olive oil.
3. Once hot, add onion, garlic. Cook 2 minutes. Add drumsticks to pot. Sear.
4. Pour in chicken broth, coconut aminos, ginger, cider vinegar, stevia. Stir.
5. Lock, seal the lid. Press "Manual" button. Cook on HIGH 9 minutes.
6. When done, naturally release pressure 5 minutes, then quick release. Remove lid.
7. Transfer drumsticks to parchment-lined baking pan. Broil in oven, 2 mins per side.
8. Press "Sauté" function on Instant Pot. Allow liquid to simmer until reduced by half.
9. Transfer drumsticks to a platter. Pour sauce over top. Garnish with fresh parsley. Serve.

Nutrition information per serving:

- Calories: 501
- Fat: 19.3g
- Carbohydrates: 4.3g
- Dietary Fiber: 0.4g
- Protein: 46g

Italian Drumsticks

Time: 29 minutes
Servings: 8
Ingredients:

- 8 skin-on chicken drumsticks
- 2 Tablespoons olive oil
- 1 medium-sized red or yellow onion, finely chopped
- 1 teaspoon chili powder
- 1 teaspoon smoked paprika or regular paprika
- 8 garlic cloves, minced
- 1 Tablespoon Italian seasoning
- 2 Tablespoons balsamic vinegar
- 3 Tablespoons dried thyme
- Pinch of salt, pepper

Marinara Sauce:

- 1 medium beet, finely chopped
- 1 pound fresh orange carrots, finely chopped
- ⅔ cup homemade low-sodium chicken broth
- 2 Tablespoons lemon juice

Instructions:

1. Season drumsticks with salt and pepper.
2. In a blender or food processor, add beets, carrots, chicken broth, lemon juice. Pulse until smooth.
3. Press "Sauté" function on Instant Pot. Add the olive oil.
4. Once hot, add onions. Sauté 3 minutes. Add garlic. Sauté 1 minute. Turn off Sauté.
5. Place drumsticks in Instant Pot. Pour in marinara sauce, chili powder, paprika, Italian seasoning, balsamic vinegar, thyme.
6. Close, seal lid. Press "Manual" button. Cook on HIGH 15 minutes.
7. When done, naturally release pressure 5 minutes, then quick release pressure. Remove lid.
8. Transfer to platter. Garnish with fresh basil. Serve.

Nutrition information per serving:

- Calories: 300
- Fat: 16.85g
- Carbohydrates: 6.89g
- Dietary Fiber: 1.8g
- Protein: 28.5g

Chicken Paprikash

Time: 25 minutes
Servings: 4
Ingredients:

- 2 pounds bone-in, skinless, chicken breasts or chicken thighs
- 1 large yellow onion, finely chopped
- 2 garlic cloves, minced
- 3 Tablespoons olive oil or coconut oil
- 1 bay leaf
- 1½ cups homemade low-sodium chicken broth
- 1 cup unsweetened coconut cream
- 3 Tablespoons paprika
- 5 Tablespoons arrowroot powder
- Juice and zest from 1 fresh lemon
- Pinch of salt, pepper

Instructions:

1. Season chicken with salt and pepper.
2. Press "Sauté" function. Add olive oil.
3. Once hot, add onion and garlic. Sauté 3 minutes.
4. Add chicken. Sear on all sides until brown.
5. Stir in chicken broth, paprika, salt, black pepper, lemon zest, lemon juice, and bay leaf to Instant Pot.
6. Close, seal lid. Press "Manual" button. Cook on HIGH 7 minutes.
7. When done, naturally release pressure 10 minutes, then quick release remaining pressure. Remove lid. Remove bay leaf.
8. Press "Sauté" function. Stir in arrowroot powder to coat ingredients. Add coconut cream. Allow to simmer until sauce thickens. Season.
9. Transfer to platter. Garnish with fresh parsley. Serve.

Nutrition information per serving:

- Calories: 720
- Fat: 43.31g
- Carbohydrates: 14.2g
- Dietary Fiber: 1.7g
- Protein: 67g

Barbecue Chicken Sliders

Time: 25 minutes
Servings: 4
Chicken Sliders:

- 4 boneless, skinless chicken breasts
- Lettuce leaves – your choice, for buns

Barbecue Sauce:

- 6 garlic cloves, minced
- 1 large yellow onion, finely chopped
- ½ cup coconut butter or ghee (clarified butter)
- 2 Tablespoons organic chili powder
- 1 Tablespoon organic cayenne pepper
- 3 cups fresh cherries, pitted and halved
- 1 apple, peeled, cored, finely chopped
- ¼ cup Swerve sweetener
- ⅓ cup Worcestershire sauce
- ¼ cup apple cider vinegar
- 3 Tablespoons organic brown mustard

Instructions:

1. Combine barbecue sauce ingredients in blender. Pulse until smooth.
2. Press "Sauté" function on Instant Pot. Add olive oil. Cook onion, garlic 3 minutes.
3. Add chicken breasts. Cover with barbecue sauce.
4. Close, seal lid. Press "Manual" button. Cook on HIGH 15 minutes.
5. When done, quick release or naturally release pressure. Carefully remove lid.
6. Transfer chicken to a cutting board, and shred using two forks.
7. Return shredded chicken to Instant Pot. Stir to coat.
8. Scoop chicken on lettuce leaves. Serve.

Nutrition information per serving:

- Calories: 820
- Fat: 50.54g
- Carbohydrates: 27.54g
- Dietary Fiber: 4.3g
- Protein: 63.32g

Chicken Carnitas

Time: 40 minutes
Servings: 6
Ingredients:

- 2 pounds boneless, skinless chicken breasts or chicken thighs
- 1 Tablespoon organic ground cumin
- 2 Tablespoons olive oil
- Juice and zest from 1 fresh orange
- ¼ cup homemade low-sodium chicken broth
- 5 garlic cloves, minced
- 1 yellow onion, finely chopped
- 1 fresh lime, juice
- 1 bay leaf
- Pinch of salt, pepper, 1 teaspoon chili powder, 1 teaspoon dried oregano
- Fresh cilantro, finely chopped
- Dressing: ½ cup homemade mayonnaise; lectin-free compliant ingredients
- 1 Tablespoon non-dairy milk; unsweetened almond or unsweetened coconut milk
- Pinch of sea salt, pinch of garlic powder
- To serve: Fresh cilantro, purple onion, tortilla shells

Instructions:

1. In a bowl, combine ingredients for dressing. Set aside.
2. In a bowl, combine cumin, chili powder, oregano, salt, pepper. Season chicken.
3. Press "Sauté" function. Add olive oil. Once hot, cook onion, garlic 3 minutes. Add chicken. Sear on all sides.
4. Add orange juice, orange zest, lime juice, chicken broth, bay leaf, cilantro.
5. Close, seal the lid. Press "Manual" button. Cook on HIGH 9 minutes.
6. When done, naturally release pressure. Remove lid. Remove bay leaf.
7. Transfer chicken to cutting board. Shred with two forks. Transfer to baking sheet. Drizzle liquid from cooking over chicken. Broil in oven 10 minutes, turn halfway.
8. Scoop chicken on tortilla shells. Garnish with purple onion, fresh cilantro, dressing. Serve.

Nutrition information per serving:

- Calories: 203
- Fat: 7.2g
- Carbohydrates: 6.21g
- Dietary Fiber: 0.9g
- Protein: 27.3g

Faux-Tisserie Whole Chicken

Time: 45 minutes
Servings: 8
Ingredients:

- 1 x 3-pound whole chicken
- 4 Tablespoons olive oil
- 6 garlic cloves, minced
- 1 lemon, quartered
- 1 cup of homemade low-sodium chicken broth
- 2 Tablespoons fresh marjoram, finely chopped
- 2 Tablespoons fresh thyme, finely chopped
- 1 Tablespoon dried basil
- 1 Tablespoon chili powder
- 1 Tablespoon onion powder
- 1 teaspoon organic ground cumin
- Pinch of salt, pepper

Instructions:

1. Drizzle light layer of oil over the chicken.
2. In a bowl, combine marjoram, thyme, basil, chili powder, onion powder, ground cumin, salt, and black pepper. Set aside.
3. Stuff garlic and lemon inside the chicken. Secure the chicken legs with string.
4. Press "Sauté" function. Once hot, place chicken in Instant Pot. Sear on all sides.
5. Sprinkle seasoning over chicken skin.
6. Pour chicken broth in Instant Pot. Set trivet in pot. Place chicken on top.
7. Close, seal the lid. Press "Manual" button. Cook on HIGH 25 minutes.
8. When done, naturally release pressure 15 minutes, then quick release pressure. Remove the lid. Transfer chicken to platter. Allow to rest 10 minutes, then remove lemon and garlic. Slice. Serve with side salad.

Nutrition information per serving:

- Calories: 483
- Fat: 33.2g
- Carbohydrates: 4.3g
- Dietary Fiber: 0.9g
- Protein: 34g

Garlic and Smoked Paprika Drumsticks

Time: 35 minutes
Servings: 10
Ingredients:

- 10 fresh chicken drumsticks or chicken legs
- Olive oil
- 2 Tablespoons smoked paprika
- 2 Tablespoons garlic powder
- Pinch of salt, pepper
- 1 cup of water

Instructions:

1. In a bowl, combine smoked paprika, garlic powder, salt, pepper. Stir.
2. Drizzle light layer of oil over chicken. Season drumsticks or legs with the spices.
3. Add 1 cup of water to Instant Pot. Place trivet in as well.
4. Place drumsticks on top of the trivet.
5. Lock, seal the lid. Press "Manual" button. Cook on HIGH 16 minutes.
6. When done, naturally release pressure 5 minutes, then quick release pressure. Remove the lid. Transfer chicken to parchment-lined baking tray.
7. Place baking tray under broiler, 2 minutes per side, until skin golden and crispy.
8. Transfer to platter. Serve.

Nutrition information per serving:

- Calories: 473
- Fat: 32g
- Carbohydrates: 3.2g
- Dietary Fiber: 0.3g
- Protein: 33.4g

Chicken Chili

Time: 28 minutes
Servings: 6
Ingredients:

- 2 pounds ground chicken
- 3 Tablespoons olive oil
- 1 medium yellow onion, finely chopped
- 4 garlic cloves, minced
- 3 fresh celery stalks, finely chopped
- 1 small can red kidney beans
- 1 small can diced tomatoes
- 2 Tablespoons organic chili powder
- 2 Tablespoons taco seasoning
- 1 Tablespoon organic ground cumin
- ½ teaspoon organic ground cinnamon
- Pinch of salt, pepper
- 2 cups homemade low-sodium chicken broth
- 1 cup vegetable broth
- Juice from 1 fresh lime
- 1 small can organic tomato puree
- For serving: fresh cilantro, avocado slices

Instructions:

1. Press "Sauté" function. Add olive oil.
2. Once hot, add onion, celery. Cook 3 minutes. Add garlic. Cook another 2 minutes.
3. Add ground chicken to pot. Cook until no longer pink.
4. Stir in chili powder, taco seasoning, cumin, cinnamon, salt, pepper.
5. Stir in tomato puree, diced tomatoes, kidney beans, vegetable broth, lime juice.
6. Close, seal the lid. Press "Manual" button. Cook on HIGH 12 minutes.
7. When done, naturally release pressure 10 minutes, then quick release pressure. Remove the lid.
8. Ladle in bowls. Garnish with fresh cilantro and avocado slices. Serve.

Nutrition information per serving:

- Calories: 395
- Fat: 12.2g
- Carbohydrates: 22.4g
- Dietary Fiber: 3.3g
- Protein: 47.2g

Fish and Seafood Recipes

Lobster Bisque Soup

Time: 20 minutes
Servings: 6
Ingredients:

- 3 cups frozen or fresh lobster meat
- 2 cups homemade low-sodium vegetable or fish broth
- 2 cups unsweetened coconut cream
- 4 Tablespoons organic ghee (clarified butter)
- 1 medium yellow or red onion, finely chopped
- 4 garlic cloves, minced
- 1 cup dry white wine
- 1 cup carrots, finely chopped
- 1 cup celery, finely chopped
- 1 Tablespoon Worcestershire sauce
- 1 teaspoon smoked paprika or regular paprika
- 1 Tablespoon fresh parsley, chopped
- 1 teaspoon dried thyme
- Pinch of salt, pepper

Instructions:

1. Press "Sauté" function on Instant Pot. Add the ghee.
2. Once melted, add onion, celery, carrots, garlic. Cook 5 minutes.
3. Deglaze Instant Pot with the wine. Simmer until reduced by half.
4. Stir in lobster meat, and broth.
5. Close, seal the lid. Press "Steam" function. Cook on HIGH 5 minutes.
6. When done, naturally release pressure. Remove the lid.
7. Stir in coconut cream, Worcestershire sauce, paprika, parsley, thyme, salt, and black pepper. Use an immersion blender to puree soup until smooth.
8. Ladle soup in bowls. Garnish with parsley, fresh ground black pepper. Serve.

Nutrition information per serving:

- Calories: 394
- Fat: 29.3g
- Carbohydrates: 5.3g
- Dietary Fiber: 0.67g
- Protein: 24.4g

Shrimp and Sausage Boil

Time: 23 minutes
Servings: 6
Ingredients:

- 1½ pounds sweet potatoes, peeled, cubed
- 1½ pounds shrimp, peeled, deveined
- 3 smoked sausage, sliced
- 1 Tablespoon low-sodium coconut aminos
- 1 Tablespoon organic Cajun or creole seasoning
- ½ cup ghee, melted
- ½ teaspoon garlic powder
- Pinch of salt, pepper
- 3 cups of homemade low-sodium fish or vegetable broth

Instructions:

1. Add sweet potato cubes, sausage to Instant Pot. Pour in broth and low-sodium coconut aminos. Stir.
2. Lock, seal the lid. Press "Manual" button. Cook on HIGH 4 minutes.
3. When done, quick release pressure. Remove the lid.
4. Add shrimp, melted ghee, garlic powder, salt, black pepper, and Cajun seasoning. Stir until well combined.
5. Allow shrimp to heat until no longer pink. Press "Sauté" function if necessary.
6. Ladle in bowls. Garnish with fresh parsley. Serve.

Nutrition information per serving:

- Calories: 663
- Fat: 38.8g
- Carbohydrates: 33.3g
- Dietary Fiber: 4.6g
7. Protein: 43.1g

Sweet Chili Tilapia

Time: 10 minutes
Servings: 4
Ingredients:

- 4 boneless, skinless tilapia fillets
- 2 teaspoons olive oil
- ¼ cup coconut aminos
- Pinch of sea salt, pepper
- 2 teaspoons crushed red pepper flakes
- Handful fresh baby spinach, finely chopped
- Topping: ¼ cup homemade lectin-free chili sauce
- 1 teaspoon organic low-sodium coconut aminos

Instructions:

1. In a bowl, combine coconut aminos, black pepper, salt, red pepper flakes, and baby spinach. Mix well. Fully coat the tilapia fillets with the marinade.
2. In a second bowl, combine chili sauce, coconut aminos. Stir well. Set aside.
3. Press "Sauté" function on Instant Pot. Set to lowest temperature.
4. Add olive oil in pot. Once hot, add tilapia fillets. Sauté for 2 to 3 minutes per side, until cooked through. Transfer fillets to serving plate. Top with chili sauce. Serve.

Nutrition information per serving:

- Calories: 118
- Fat: 3.4g
- Carbohydrates: 1g
- Dietary Fiber: 0g
- Protein: 21.1g

Ginger Tilapia

Time: 23 minutes
Servings: 4
Ingredients:

- 1 pound tilapia fish fillets
- 3 Tablespoons low-sodium coconut aminos
- 2 Tablespoons white vinegar or apple cider
- 2 fresh garlic cloves, finely minced
- Pinch of salt, white pepper
- 1 Tablespoon olive oil
- 2 Tablespoons fresh ginger, julienned
- ¼ cup fresh scallions, julienned
- ¼ cup fresh cilantro, finely chopped

Instructions:

1. In a bowl, combine coconut aminos, white vinegar, minced garlic, salt, white pepper. Mix well.
2. Add tilapia fish. Gently spoon sauce over fish to coat evenly. Marinate 2 hours.
3. Add 2 cups water, and a steamer rack to the Instant Pot.
4. Remove fillets from marinade, place on steamer rack. Reserve marinade.
5. Close, seal the lid. Press "Manual" button. Cook on LOW 2 minutes.
6. When done, quick release pressure. Remove the lid.
7. Transfer fillets to serving dish. Discard the water.
8. Press "Sauté" function on Instant Pot. Add olive oil. Once hot, add julienned ginger, sauté a few seconds. Add scallions, cilantro. Sauté 2 minutes, until soft.
9. Stir in reserved marinade, allow to heat through. Spoon sauce over the fish. Serve.

Nutrition information per serving:

- Calories: 176
- Fat: 6g
- Carbohydrates: 4.98g
- Dietary Fiber: 0.53g
- Protein: 25g

Steamed Crab Legs

Time: 5 minutes
Servings: 4
Ingredients:

- 2 pounds cleaned snow crab legs
- Juice and zest from 1 medium fresh lemon
- ½ cup organic apple cider or white vinegar
- 2 Tablespoons ghee or coconut oil, melted
- 1 teaspoon smoked paprika or regular paprika
- Pinch of sea salt, white pepper
- 4 garlic cloves, crushed
- 2 cups of water
- Fresh parsley

Instructions:

1. In a bowl, combine lemon juice, lemon zest, apple cider, crushed garlic, ghee, paprika, salt, and black pepper. Mix well.
2. Add 2 cups of water to Instant Pot. Place steamer rack in pot.
3. Add snow crab legs on steamer rack. Drizzle with the lemon mixture.
4. Lock, seal the lid. Press "Manual" button. Cook on HIGH 2 minutes.
5. When done, quick release pressure. Remove the lid.
6. Transfer to serving platter. Garnish with fresh parsley.

Nutrition information per serving:

- Calories: 176
- Fat: 7.9g
- Carbohydrates: 5g
- Dietary Fiber: 0.4g
- Protein: 19.2g

Lemon Salmon

Time: 16 minutes
Servings: 4
Ingredients:

- 1 pound skin-on salmon fillets
- 1 Tablespoon ghee, melted
- Pinch of salt, white pepper
- ½ medium fresh lemon, thinly sliced
- Sprigs of fresh dill, fresh parsley, fresh tarragon, fresh basil
- 1 cup of water

Instructions:

1. Add 1 cup water, herbs, and a steamer rack to Instant Pot.
2. Season salmon with salt, white pepper. Drizzle with melted ghee.
3. Place fillets on steamer rack. Top with lemon slices.
4. Close, seal the lid. Press "Steam" button. Cook on HIGH 3 minutes.
5. When done, manually release pressure. Remove the lid.
6. Transfer to platter. Garnish with fresh herbs. Serve.

Nutrition information per serving:

- Calories: 180
- Fat: 10.2g
- Carbohydrates: 0.7g
- Dietary Fiber: 0.2g
- Protein: 22.1g

Chili-Lime Halibut

Time: 15 minutes
Servings: 2
Ingredients:

- 2 x 5-ouunce halibut fillets
- 1 cup of water
- Pinch of sea salt, pepper

Chili-Lime Sauce Ingredients:

- 1 medium jalapeno, seeded, peeled, finely chopped
- Juice from 1 fresh lime
- 2 garlic cloves, finely minced
- 1 Tablespoon melted coconut oil
- 1 Tablespoon freshly chopped parsley
- ½ teaspoon organic cumin
- 1 teaspoon organic smoked paprika
- Small pinch of sea salt

Instructions:

1. In a bowl, combine chili lime sauce ingredients. Stir well. Set aside.
2. Add 1 cup of water, and steamer rack to your Instant Pot.
3. Season halibut fillets with salt and pepper. Place fillets on top of steamer rack.
4. Lock, seal the lid. Press "Steam" setting. Cook on HIGH 5 minutes.
5. When done, manually release pressure. Remove the lid.
6. Transfer fillets to serving dish. Drizzle with chili sauce. Serve.

Nutrition information per serving:

- Calories: 419
- Fat: 25.56g
- Carbohydrates: 15.06g
- Dietary Fiber: 8.9g
- Protein: 32.75g

Cajun Tilapia

Time: 13 minutes
Servings: 4
Ingredients:

- 4 x 6-ounce tilapia fillets
- 1 cup ghee or non-dairy butter, melted
- 2 teaspoons cayenne pepper
- 2 Tablespoons smoked paprika
- 2 teaspoons garlic powder
- 2 teaspoons onion powder
- Pinch of salt, pepper
- 1 teaspoon dried oregano
- 1 teaspoon dried thyme
- 1 cup of water

Instructions:

1. In a small bowl, combine cayenne pepper, smoked paprika, garlic powder, onion powder, salt, pepper, dried oregano, and dried thyme. Add melted ghee. Mix well.
2. Dip each tilapia fillet in seasoned ghee.
3. Add 1 cup of water, and steamer rack to Instant Pot. Place seasoned fillets on rack.
4. Close, seal lid. Press "Manual" button. Cook on HIGH 5 minutes.
5. When done, manually release pressure. Remove the lid.
6. Transfer to platter. Garnish with fresh parsley, lemon wedges. Serve.

Nutrition information per serving:

- Calories: 383
- Fat: 26g
- Carbohydrates: 9.31g
- Dietary Fiber: 0.98g
- Protein: 28.93g

Spicy Shrimp and Cauliflower Grits

Time: 25 minutes
Servings: 4
Cauliflower Grits Ingredients:

- 4 cups grated cauliflower
- 1 cup unsweetened coconut milk
- 1 Tablespoon ghee or non-dairy butter
- ¼ cup homemade low-sodium chicken broth
- 1 teaspoon olive oil
- Pinch of salt

Shrimp Ingredients:

- 1 pound shrimp, peeled and deveined
- Pinch of sea salt, pepper
- ¼ teaspoon cayenne pepper
- ¼ teaspoon paprika
- 4 bacon slices, finely chopped
- ¼ cup onion, finely chopped
- 2 Tablespoons olive oil
- 1 Tablespoon fresh lemon juice
- Garnish: green onions, 8 cups fresh swiss chard, sliced

Instructions:

1. Press "Sauté" function on Instant Pot. Add 1 teaspoon of olive oil.
2. Once hot, add grated cauliflower. Toast 3 minutes, stirring frequently. Turn off "Sauté" function. Add remaining grit ingredients. Stir.
3. In a bowl, combine shrimp ingredients. Stir well. Place shrimp on top of grits.
4. Lock, seal the lid. Press "Manual" button. Cook on HIGH 10 minutes.
5. When done, naturally release pressure 10 minutes. Remove the lid.
6. In a serving dish or serving platter, add the swiss chard. Top with grits and shrimp. Garnish with green onions. Serve.

Nutrition information per serving:

- Calories: 368
- Fat: 23.68g
- Carbohydrates: 8.46g
- Dietary Fiber: 2.1g
- Protein: 30.42g

Lemon-Dill Salmon Fillet

Time: 20 minutes
Servings: 4
Ingredients:

- 1 cup of water
- 1 pound organic wild-caught salmon fillet
- 3 Tablespoons of ghee.
- 2 garlic cloves, minced
- 5 large fresh sprigs of dill
- 2 medium lemon, thinly sliced
- 12 asparagus, trimmed, sliced into 1-inch pieces
- Pinch of salt, pepper

Instructions:

1. Drizzle ghee over both sides of salmon. Season with salt, pepper.
2. Add water, fresh dill, and minced garlic to Instant Pot Add a trivet to pot.
3. Place salmon on top of trivet. Layer lemon slices over salmon fillet.
4. Close, seal the lid. Press "Manual" button. Cook on HIGH 4 minutes.
5. When done, quick release pressure. Remove the lid.
6. Transfer salmon to serving platter. Remove the trivet and discard the liquid.
7. Press "Sauté" function on Instant Pot. Add remaining 2 Tablespoons of ghee.
8. Add asparagus. Cook 4 minutes, season with salt and pepper.
9. Cut the salmon into 4 pieces, serve with asparagus.

Nutrition information per serving:

- Calories: 260
- Fat: 16.7g
- Carbohydrates: 5.4g
- Dietary Fiber: 2.7g
- Protein: 24.6g

Pork Recipes

Pork and Cabbage Bowl

Time: 15 minutes
Servings: 6
Ingredients:

- 1½ pounds ground pork
- 2 Tablespoons olive oil
- 2 shallots, peeled, finely chopped
- 1 cup homemade low-sodium chicken broth
- 2 cups cauliflower florets, finely chopped
- 6 cups fresh green cabbage, finely shredded
- 2 garlic cloves, minced
- Pinch of salt, pepper

Instructions:

1. Press "Sauté" function on Instant Pot. Add the olive oil.
2. Once hot, add ground pork, finely chopped shallots, and minced garlic. Cook until pork is browned, stirring occasionally. Turn off "Sauté" function.
3. Add cauliflower, cabbage, salt, and black pepper to Instant Pot.
4. Close, seal the lid. Press "Manual" button. Cook on HIGH 3 minutes.
5. When done, quick release pressure. Remove the lid.
6. Transfer to platter. Serve.

Nutrition information per serving:

- Calories: 163
- Fat: 4g
- Carbohydrates: 8.6g
- Dietary Fiber: 3.85g
- Protein: 21g

Italian Pork Stuffed Sweet Potatoes

Time: 28 minutes
Servings: 2
Ingredients:

- 1 pound lean grass-fed ground pork
- 2 medium sweet potatoes
- 2 cups of water
- 1 medium yellow onion, finely chopped
- 2 Tablespoons olive oil
- 4 cups fresh kale, roughly chopped
- 1 Tablespoon fresh parsley, finely chopped
- 1 teaspoon garlic powder
- Pinch of salt, pepper

Instructions:

1. Add 2 cups of water, and trivet to Instant Pot. Place sweet potatoes on top of trivet.
2. Close, seal the lid. Press "Manual" button. Cook on HIGH 15 minutes.
3. When done, naturally release pressure 10 minutes. Remove the lid. Remove sweet potatoes from Instant Pot. Discard the water and trivet.
4. Press "Sauté" function on Instant Pot. Add the olive oil.
5. Once hot, add ground pork, onion, parsley, garlic powder, salt, pepper. Stir.
6. Add the kale, cook until wilted, stirring occasionally. Turn off "Sauté" function.
7. Cut sweet potatoes in half. Scoop out potato. Fill with ground pork mixture. Serve.

Nutrition information per serving:

- Calories: 517
- Fat: 21.2g
- Carbohydrates: 38.12g
- Dietary Fiber: 4.8g
- Protein: 33.12g

Pulled Pork Soup

Time: 45 minutes
Servings: 6
Ingredients:

- 1½ pound organic boneless whole pork shoulder
- 2 Tablespoons olive oil
- 1½ pounds organic cauliflower florets
- 7 cups homemade low-sodium chicken or pork broth
- 8 garlic cloves, minced
- 1 large red onion, diced
- ½ cup unsweetened coconut cream
- Pinch of salt, pepper

Instructions:

1. Press "Sauté" function. Add 1 tablespoon olive oil.
2. Once hot, add pork shoulder. Sear on all sides.
3. Add remaining tablespoon olive oil. Once hot, add onion, and garlic cloves. Cook 5 minutes. Add broth, salt, pepper, cauliflower. Stir.
4. Lock, the lid. Press "Manual" button. Cook on HIGH 45 minutes.
5. When done, naturally release pressure 10 minutes, then quick release remaining pressure. Remove the lid.
6. Transfer pork shoulder to cutting board. Shred using two forks.
7. Using an immersion blender, pulse cauliflower mixture in Instant Pot until smooth. Stir in pulled pork, and coconut cream. Season as needed.
8. Ladle in bowls. Serve.

Nutrition information per serving:

- Calories: 409
- Fat: 24.6g
- Carbohydrates: 14.8g
- Dietary Fiber: 5g
- Protein: 34g

Pork Chops with Red Cabbage

Time: 22 minutes
Servings: 4
Ingredients:

- 4 pork chops
- 1 small head of red cabbage, cored, shredded
- 1 Tablespoon olive oil
- 2 cups homemade low-sodium chicken broth
- 3 Tablespoons arrowroot powder
- 1 teaspoon garlic powder
- 1 teaspoon onion powder
- 1 Tablespoon freshly chopped parsley
- 2 teaspoons dried thyme
- Pinch of salt, pepper
- 1 teaspoon fennel seeds

Instructions:

1. In a bowl, combine garlic powder, onion powder, parsley, dried thyme, salt, black pepper, and fennel seeds. Season pork with spices.
2. Press "Sauté" function on Instant Pot. Add the olive oil.
3. Once hot, add pork chops. Sear on both sides. Remove and set aside.
4. Add shredded cabbage, and chicken stock to Instant Pot. Stir.
5. Place pork chops on top of cabbage.
6. Close, seal the lid. Press "Manual" button. Cook on HIGH 8 minutes.
7. When done, quick release pressure. Remove the lid.
8. Transfer cabbage and pork chops to a serving platter.
9. Press "Sauté" function on Instant Pot. Stir in arrowroot powder. Simmer until thickened, stirring occasionally. Pour sauce over cabbage and pork. Serve.

Nutrition information per serving:

- Calories: 369
- Fat: 23.6g
- Carbohydrates: 19.2g
- Dietary Fiber: 5.7g
- Protein: 20.9g

Swedish-Inspired Pork Roast

Time: 1 hour and 30 minutes
Servings: 8
Ingredients:

- 4 pounds boneless pork loin roast
- 1 Tablespoon olive oil
- 2 cups homemade low-sodium beef broth
- 1 large yellow onion, peeled, grated
- 8 garlic cloves, crushed
- 3 Tablespoons of swerve or Erythritol sweetener
- 2 Tablespoons sea salt
- 1 Tablespoon fresh parsley, finely chopped
- 1 teaspoon organic ground cumin powder
- ½ teaspoon organic ground cardamom powder
- 1 teaspoon fresh ground nutmeg
- 1 teaspoon freshly cracked black pepper.

Instructions:

1. Season pork loin roast with swerve, salt, cumin powder, cardamom powder, pepper.
2. Press "Sauté" function on Instant Pot. Add the olive oil.
3. Once hot, add onion, garlic. Cook 4 minutes.
4. Add pork roast. Sear on all sides. Stir in beef broth.
5. Lock, seal the lid. Press "Manual" button. Cook on HIGH 85 minutes.
6. When done, naturally release pressure. Remove the lid.
7. Transfer roast to serving platter. Allow to rest 10 minutes before slicing. Ladle liquid over slices. Serve.

Nutrition information per serving:

- Calories: 287
- Fat: 6.7g
- Carbohydrates: 5.5g
- Dietary Fiber: 0.3g
- Protein: 48.7g

Hawaiian Kalua Pork

Time: 1 hour and 30 minutes
Servings: 8
Ingredients:

- 1 (5-pound) bone-in or boneless pork shoulder, cut into 3 pieces
- 1 (20-ounce) can of pineapple chunks in pineapple juice
- 3 whole garlic cloves
- 6 bacon slices
- 1 cup of homemade low-sodium beef broth or beef stock
- 1 medium-sized green cabbage, cored and into six wedges
- 1 ½ Tablespoon of sea salt
- 1 teaspoon of freshly cracked black pepper.

Instructions:

1. Press the "Sauté" function on your Instant Pot and add the bacon slices. Cook brown on both sides. Turn off "Sauté" function on your Instant Pot.
2. Make an incision in the pork pieces and insert the whole garlic cloves.
3. Sprinkle with salt and black pepper. Place the pork pieces on top of the bacon and pour in the beef broth and pineapple juice.
4. Lock the lid and ensure the valve is closed. Press the "Manual" button and cook for 90 minutes on High Pressure.
5. When the cooking is done, naturally release the pressure and remove the lid.
6. Transfer the pork and bacon to a serving platter and shred using two forks.
7. Add the cabbage wedges and pineapple chunks to your Instant Pot.
8. Close the lid and cook for 3 minutes on High Pressure.
9. When the cooking is done, quick release the pressure and remove the lid.
10. Place the pineapple cabbage on top of the shredded pork.
11. Serve and enjoy!

Nutrition information per serving:

- Calories: 518
- Fat: 16g
- Carbohydrates: 9.5g
- Dietary Fiber: 1g
- Protein: 79.9g

Spicy Spinach and Pork Stew

Time: 40 minutes   Servings: 4

Ingredients:

- 1 pound boneless pork stewing meat, cut into bite-sized pieces
- 1 large red onion, peeled, finely chopped
- 4 garlic cloves, minced
- 1½ cups homemade low-sodium vegetable broth
- 1 teaspoon dried thyme
- Pinch of sea salt, pepper
- ½ cup organic heavy cream
- 6 cups fresh baby spinach, coarsely chopped

Instructions:

1. In a blender/food processor, combine onion, garlic, vegetable broth until smooth.
2. Add mixture to Instant Pot, along with pork pieces.
3. Close, seal the lid. Press "Manual" button. Cook on HIGH 20 minutes.
4. When done, naturally release pressure. Remove the lid.
5. Press "Sauté" function. Stir in salt, dried thyme, pepper, heavy cream, and baby spinach. Cook until spinach wilts, stirring frequently.
6. Transfer to platter. Serve.

Nutrition information per serving:

- Calories: 295
- Fat: 16.35g
- Carbohydrates: 9.23g
- Dietary Fiber: 1.98g
- Protein: 24g

Tender Ribs

Time: 1 hour   Servings: 8

Ingredients:

- 2 racks pork ribs
- 1 cup of water
- ¼ cup of apple cider vinegar
- 1 Tablespoon low-sodium coconut aminos
- 1 Tablespoon Worcestershire sauce
- Pinch of salt, pepper
- 1 teaspoon garlic powder
- 1 teaspoon chili powder
- 1 teaspoon onion powder
- 1 teaspoon paprika

Instructions:

1. Season pork ribs with salt, black pepper, garlic powder, onion powder, chili powder, and paprika.
2. Place a trivet in Instant pot. Add water, apple cider vinegar, and coconut aminos.
3. Place the ribs on the trivet. Lock, seal the lid.
4. Press "Manual" button. Cook on HIGH 25 minutes.
5. When done, naturally release pressure. Remove the lid.
6. Transfer ribs to platter. Allow to rest 10 minutes. Serve.

Nutrition information per serving:

- Calories: 475
- Fat: 25.08g
- Carbohydrates: 0g
- Dietary Fiber: 0g
- Protein: 58.08g

Adobo Pork

Time: 1 hour
Servings: 6
Ingredients:

- 2 pounds boneless pork shoulder
- 1 Tablespoon Adobo seasoning
- 1 Tablespoon turmeric
- Pinch of salt, pepper
- ½ pound green chilies, de-seeded
- ½ pound organic red Fresno peppers or red jalapenos
- 2 garlic cloves, crushed
- 1 teaspoon swerve or Erythritol
- 2 teaspoons apple cider vinegar
- ½ cup homemade low-sodium chicken broth or water

Instructions:

1. In a blender or food processor, combine green chilies, red peppers, garlic cloves, swerve, apple cider vinegar, and chicken broth. Pulse until smooth.
2. In a bowl, combine adobo seasoning, turmeric, salt, and pepper. Season pork on all sides. Add pork shoulder to Instant Pot. Pour the sauce over roast.
3. Lock, seal the lid. Select "Manual" setting. Cook on HIGH 45 minutes.
4. When done, naturally release pressure. Remove the lid.
5. Transfer pork to serving platter. Shred with two forks.
6. Return to pot. Coat with sauce. Serve.

Nutrition information per serving:

- Calories: 240
- Fat: 5.5g
- Carbohydrates: 4.8g
- Dietary Fiber: 1.1g
- Protein: 40.1g

Orange Shredded Pork

Time: 1 hour and 30 minutes
Servings: 8
Ingredients:

- 3 pounds boneless pork butt, cut into3 equal sized pieces
- 1½ cups fresh orange juice
- 1 medium sweet onion, finely chopped
- 4 dried ancho chilies, stemmed, seeded
- 4 garlic cloves, minced
- ⅔ cups organic apple cider vinegar
- ½ cup fresh parsley, finely chopped
- 1 teaspoon dried oregano
- ½ teaspoon organic ground cumin
- Pinch of sea salt, pepper

Instructions:

1. Add the orange juice and pork pieces to your Instant Pot.
2. Lock, seal the lid. Press "Manual" button. Cook on HIGH 50 minutes at.
3. When done, naturally release pressure. Remove the lid.
4. Transfer pork pieces to a serving platter. Shred using two forks. Set aside.
5. In a blender, combine onion, ancho chilies, garlic cloves, apple cider vinegar, parsley, oregano, ground cumin, salt, and black pepper. Blend until smooth.
6. Press "Sauté" function on Instant Pot. Set to low. Pour in sauce. Simmer couple of minutes until thickens, stirring occasionally.
7. Stir in shredded pork to coat evenly. Transfer to platter. Serve.

Nutrition information per serving:

- Calories: 295
- Fat: 6.1g
- Carbohydrates: 9.5g
- Dietary Fiber: 1.1g
- Protein: 45.9g

Beef Recipes

Chuck Roast Stew

Time: 35 minutes
Servings: 8
Ingredients:

- ½ pounds organic bacon strips, finely chopped
- 3 pounds lean grass-fed chuck roast, cut into bite-sized pieces
- 2 Tablespoons olive oil
- 2 carrots, thinly sliced
- 2 celery ribs, chopped
- 1 sweet potato, cubed
- 2 large red onions, sliced
- 3 garlic cloves, crushed
- 1 small purple cabbage, cored and shredded
- 1 cup homemade low-sodium beef broth
- 1 Tablespoon Worcestershire sauce
- 2 Tablespoons arrowroot powder
- Pinch of salt, pepper

Instructions:

1. Press "Sauté" function on Instant Pot. Once hot, cook bacon until brown. Remove from pot. Set aside. Continue in "Sauté," add chuck roast pieces, sear on all sides. Remove from pot. Set aside.
2. Add onion, garlic, celery, carrots, sweet potatoes to Instant Pot. Cook 5 minutes.
3. Return beef, bacon to pot. Add broth, cabbage, Worcestershire sauce, salt, pepper.
4. Lock, seal the lid. Press "Manual" button. Cook on HIGH 28 minutes.
5. When done, naturally release pressure. Remove the lid. Transfer roast pieces to bowl. Press "Sauté" function. Sprinkle in arrowroot powder. Simmer liquid until thickens. Return pieces to pot. Stir to coat evenly. Transfer to platter. Serve.

Nutrition information per serving:

- Calories: 375
- Fat: 23.2g
- Carbohydrates: 5.83g
- Dietary Fiber: 2g
- Protein: 38g

Beef Meatballs with Mushroom Sauce

Time: 24 minutes
Servings: 6
Ingredients:

- 2 pounds lean grass-fed ground beef
- 1 yellow onion, finely chopped
- 1 medium carrot, grated
- 2 large eggs
- 2 Tablespoons arrowroot powder
- 2 Tablespoons mustard
- 1 Tablespoon dried oregano
- ¼ cup fresh parsley, chopped
- 1 Tablespoon smoked or regular paprika
- Pinch of salt, pepper
- 2 cups homemade low-sodium beef broth
- 2 cups mushrooms
- ½ cup unsweetened coconut cream
- 2 Tablespoons olive oil

Instructions:

1. In a large bowl, add ground beef, onion, grated carrots, egg, arrowroot powder mustard, dried oregano, paprika, salt, and black pepper. Stir until combined.
2. Form ground beef mixture into meatballs. Set aside.
3. Press "Sauté" function on Instant Pot. Add the olive oil.
4. Once hot, place single layer of meatballs in pot. Cook until brown on all sides.
5. Pour beef broth, and mushrooms.
6. Close, seal the lid. Press "Manual" button. Cook on HIGH 16 minutes.
7. When done, naturally release pressure 10 minutes. Remove the lid.
8. Transfer meatballs to serving platter.
9. Use an immersion blender to pulse mushrooms until smooth. Stir in coconut cream, and parsley. Ladle mushroom sauce over meatballs. Serve.

Nutrition information per serving:

- Calories: 514
- Fat: 32.07g
- Carbohydrates: 8.06g
- Dietary Fiber: 1.4g
- Protein: 46.88g

Fajita Steak Bowl

Time: 17 minutes
Servings: 6
Ingredients:

- 2½ pounds organic fajita steak, cut into bite-sized pieces
- 4 avocados, peeled, nut removed, diced
- 2 Tablespoons olive oil
- 4 garlic cloves, minced
- 1 teaspoon chili powder
- 1 Tablespoon fresh lime juice
- 1 cup organic low-sodium beef broth
- Pinch of salt, pepper

Instructions:

1. Press "Sauté" function on Instant Pot. Add the olive oil.
2. Once hot, add garlic and sauté 2 minutes.
3. Add steak pieces. Cook until almost brown.
4. Add remaining ingredients. Stir well.
5. Lock, seal the lid. Press "Manual" button. Cook on HIGH 10 minutes.
6. When done, quick release pressure. Remove the lid.
7. Press "Sauté" function. Simmer until most of liquid evaporates.
8. Transfer steak pieces to a bowl with diced avocado. Serve.

Nutrition information per serving:

- Calories: 603
- Fat: 40.3g
- Carbohydrates: 13.5g
- Dietary Fiber: 9.1g
- Protein: 48.8g

Easy Taco Meat

Time: 15 minutes
Servings: 6
Ingredients:

- 2 pounds organic, lean, grass-fed ground beef
- 4 Tablespoons olive oil or coconut oil
- 2 medium organic red onions, finely chopped
- 6 garlic cloves, minced
- 1 Tablespoon chili powder
- 1 Tablespoon dried oregano
- 1 Tablespoon dried basil
- ⅓ cup fresh cilantro, finely chopped
- 1 teaspoon regular paprika or smoked paprika
- 1 teaspoon cumin
- Pinch of salt, pepper

Instructions:

1. Press "Sauté" function on Instant Pot. Add the oil.
2. Once hot, add onion. Cook 3 minutes. Add garlic. Cook 2 minutes. Add ground beef. Cook until brown, stirring occasionally.
3. Add remaining ingredients, except cilantro. Stir well.
4. Lock, seal the lid. Press "Manual" button. Cook on HIGH 9 minutes.
5. When done, naturally release pressure. Remove the lid.
6. Press "Sauté" function. Simmer until most of liquid is reduced.
7. Transfer to bowl. Garnish with fresh cilantro. Serve.

Nutrition information per serving:

- Calories: 442
- Fat: 34.2g
- Carbohydrates: 6.3g
- Dietary Fiber: 1.84g
- Protein: 29.1g

Beef Burgundy with Mushrooms

Time: 43 minutes
Servings: 6
Ingredients:

- 2 pounds organic beef chuck roast, cut into bite-sized pieces
- 3 Tablespoons almond flour
- 3 Tablespoons olive oil, avocado oil, or coconut oil
- 4 garlic cloves, minced
- 1 yellow onion, finely chopped
- 1 cup of red wine
- ½ cup homemade low-sodium beef broth
- 1 teaspoon fresh thyme
- 4 carrots, peeled, cut into bite-sized pieces
- 1 ½ cups mushrooms, sliced
- 2 bay leaves
- Pinch of salt, pepper

Instructions:

1. Season beef pieces with salt, pepper. Lightly coat with almond flour.
2. Press "Sauté" function on Instant Pot. Add the olive oil.
3. Once hot, add onions. Cook 3 minutes. Add garlic. Cook 2 minutes. Add beef pieces. Sear on all sides. Remove and set aside.
4. Deglaze Instant Pot with red wine. Scrape up any brown bits along bottom. Simmer, reduce wine by half.
5. Return beef to Instant Pot. Stir in broth, thyme, carrots, mushroom, bay leaves.
6. Lock, seal the lid. Press "Manual" button. Cook on HIGH 40 minutes.
7. When done, naturally release pressure 10 minutes, then quick release remaining pressure. Remove the lid. Remove bay leaves.
8. Season. Transfer to platter. Serve.

Nutrition information per serving:

- Calories: 288
- Fat: 15.89g
- Carbohydrates: 5.07g
- Dietary Fiber: 1.5g
- Protein: 35g

Garlic and Rosemary Rib Eye Roast

Time: 1 hour
Servings: 6
Ingredients:

- 1 x 3-pound boneless organic rib eye beef roast, cut into large pieces
- 4 medium onions, sliced
- 10 garlic cloves, minced
- 4 Tablespoons olive oil
- 4 Tablespoons ghee, melted
- 4 cups mushrooms, sliced
- ¼ cup fresh rosemary
- ¼ cup fresh parsley, finely chopped
- Pinch of salt, pepper
- 2 cups homemade beef broth or water

Instructions:

1. Season beef chunks with salt and pepper.
2. In a bowl, combine parsley, rosemary, garlic, and melted ghee. Mix well.
3. Press "Sauté" function on Instant Pot. Add 2 tablespoons of olive oil.
4. Add beef pieces. Sear on all sides. Transfer beef pieces to a cutting board, brush with garlic and herb mixture.
5. Add remaining 2 tablespoons olive oil with sliced onions. Cook until lightly browned, stirring occasionally. Turn off "Sauté" function on Instant Pot.
6. Add mushrooms and beef broth to Instant Pot. Return beef roast pieces to pot.
7. Lock, seal the lid. Press "Manual" button. Cook on HIGH 40 minutes.
8. When done, naturally release pressure. Remove the lid.
9. Remove beef from Instant Pot. Transfer to platter.
10. Use an immersion blender to puree sauce. Pour over beef chunks. Serve.

Nutrition information per serving:

- Calories: 445
- Fat: 22g
- Carbohydrates: 11g
- Dietary Fiber: 2g
- Protein: 52g

Beef Curry

Time: 46 minutes
Servings: 6
Ingredients:

- 1 pound organic grass-fed boneless beef stewing meat, cut into bite-sized pieces
- 2 Tablespoons coconut oil, olive oil, or ghee
- 1 onion, finely chopped
- 3 large sweet potatoes, cubed
- 6 carrots, peeled and cut into bite-sized pieces
- 4 garlic cloves, minced
- 2 Tablespoons of curry powder
- Pinch of salt, pepper
- 1 teaspoon dried oregano
- 1 teaspoon paprika
- 1 cup unsweetened coconut cream
- ½ cup homemade low-sodium bone broth
- 2 Tablespoons arrowroot powder

Instructions:

1. Press the "Sauté" function on your Instant Pot and add the cooking oil.
2. Once hot, add onions and garlic. Sauté until lightly browned, stirring occasionally.
3. Add beef stewing meat to Instant Pot. Cook until brown on all sides, stirring occasionally. Turn off the "Sauté" function.
4. Stir in carrots, curry powder, salt, black pepper, dried oregano, paprika, coconut cream, and bone broth.
5. Lock, seal the lid. Press "Manual" button. Cook on HIGH 30 minutes.
6. When done, quick release or naturally release pressure. Remove the lid.
7. Transfer meat to platter. Stir in arrowroot powder. Simmer to thicken. Return meat to sauce. Stir to coat. Transfer to platter. Garnish with fresh celery. Serve.

Nutrition information per serving:

- Calories: 398
- Fat: 25.7g
- Carbohydrates: 13.3g
- Dietary Fiber: 4g
- Protein: 29g

Wine and Coffee Beef Stew

Time: 30 minutes
Servings: 8
Ingredients:

- 2½ pounds organic grass-fed beef chuck stew meat, cut into bite-sized chunks
- 3 Tablespoons olive oil, coconut oil, avocado oil, or ghee
- 2 Tablespoons organic capers
- 2 garlic cloves, minced
- 3 cups of homemade freshly brewed coffee
- 1 cup of homemade organic low-sodium beef bone broth
- 2 cups of fresh organic mushrooms, sliced
- ⅔ cups organic red cooking wine
- 1 medium onion, finely chopped
- 2 Tablespoons arrowroot powder
- Pinch of salt, pepper

Instructions:

1. Press "Saute" function on Instant Pot. Add the oil.
2. Once hot, working in batches if necessary, add stewing beef, sear on all sides. Remove and set aside.
3. Add garlic, onion, and mushrooms to Instant Pot. Cook until lightly softened, stirring occasionally. Turn off "Sauté" function on your Instant Pot.
4. Return browned stew meat. Stir in capers, brewed coffee, beef broth, red cooking wine, salt, and pepper.
5. Lock, seal the lid. Press "Manual" button. Cook on HIGH 25 minutes.
6. When done, allow full natural release. Remove the lid.
7. Press "Sauté" function on Instant Pot. Sprinkle the arrowroot powder and allow to simmer until the liquid is reduced and thickens. Transfer beef back to Instant Pot. Stir to coat. Transfer to platter. Serve.

Nutrition information per serving:

- Calories: 242
- Fat: 13.28g
- Carbohydrates: 1.35g
- Dietary Fiber: 0.3g
- Protein: 30.13g

Meatloaf with Pumpkin Barbecue Sauce

Time: 33 minutes
Servings: 8
Meatloaf Ingredients:

- 2½ pounds of organic grass-fed lean ground beef
- 1 cup organic pureed pumpkins
- ½ red onion, finely chopped
- 2 eggs
- 3 garlic cloves, minced
- 1 Tablespoon smoked paprika
- Pinch of salt, pepper
- 1 teaspoon organic cinnamon powder
- 1 teaspoon chili powder

Pumpkin Barbecue Glaze Ingredients:

- 1 cup organic pureed pumpkins
- 2 Tablespoons Worcestershire sauce
- 2 Tablespoons organic lectin-free mustard
- 2 Tablespoons apple cider vinegar
- ½ cup molasses
- 1 Tablespoon parsley, oregano, or thyme, ½ teaspoon of salt
- 2 teaspoons organic ground cinnamon powder

Instructions:

1. In a bowl, add and mix all the pumpkin barbecue glaze ingredients until well combined. Set aside.
2. In another large bowl, add meatloaf ingredients. Stir until well combined.
3. Form beef mixture into a loaf, and place on a sheet of aluminum foil. Pour pumpkin sauce over meatloaf. Fold aluminum foil over meatloaf.
4. Add 1 cup of water, and trivet to Instant Pot. Place meatloaf on top of trivet.
5. Lock, seal the lid. Press "Manual" button. Cook on HIGH 20 minutes.
6. When done, quick release pressure. Remove the lid.
7. Remove meatloaf from foil. Allow to rest 5 minutes before slicing. Serve.

Nutrition information per serving:

- Calories: 489
- Fat: 26.61g
- Carbohydrates: 20.33g
- Dietary Fiber: 1.9g
- Protein: 45.95g

Sloppy Joes

Time: 16 minutes
Servings: 4
Ingredients:

- 2½ pounds organic grass-fed lean ground beef
- 1 large onion, finely chopped
- 2 Tablespoons olive oil
- ¼ cup Worcestershire sauce
- ¼ cup low-sodium coconut aminos
- 1 teaspoon chili powder, 1 teaspoon paprika, Pinch of salt, pepper
- ¼ cup red wine vinegar
- Sauce ingredients: 1 x 8-ounce can of beets
- 1 cup organic pumpkin puree, 1 Tablespoon balsamic vinegar
- 2 Tablespoons fresh lime juice, 1 cup carrots, diced
- 4 garlic cloves, minced, 1 cup chicken broth or water
- ⅓ cup dried basil, ⅓ cup dried parsley

Instructions:

1. Add sloppy joe sauce ingredients to blender/food processor. Blend until smooth.
2. Press "Sauté" function on Instant Pot. Add the olive oil.
3. Once hot, add onions. Cook 4 minutes.
4. Add ground beef to Instant Pot. Cook until no longer pink, stirring occasionally.
5. Stir in Worcestershire sauce, coconut aminos, chili powder, paprika, red wine vinegar, salt, and black pepper.
6. Lock, seal the lid. Press "Manual" button. Cook on HIGH 3 minutes.
7. When done, naturally release pressure 15 minutes, then quick release remaining pressure. Remove the lid.
8. Press "Sauté" function. Simmer until liquid reduces. Transfer to platter. Serve.

Nutrition information per serving:

- Calories: 437
- Fat: 25.03g
- Carbohydrates: 11.23g
- Dietary Fiber: 2.8g
- Protein: 45.15g

Lamb Recipes

Greek-Style Ground Lamb Gyros

Time: 50 minutes
Servings: 6
Ingredients:

- 2 pounds lean organic ground lamb
- 1 small yellow onion, finely chopped
- 8 whole garlic cloves
- 1 Tablespoon organic ground marjoram
- 1 Tablespoon dried or fresh rosemary
- 1 Tablespoon dried or fresh oregano
- Pinch salt, pepper

Instructions:

1. In a food processor, add the onions, garlic, ground marjoram, rosemary, oregano, black pepper, and salt. Process until finely minced.
2. Transfer mixture to a large bowl. Add ground lamb and stir until well combined.
3. Press ground lamb mixture to a greased loaf pan; that can fit inside your Instant Pot. Tightly cover with aluminum foil.
4. Add 2 cups of water, and trivet to your Instant Pot. Place the loaf pan on top.
5. Lock, seal the lid. Press "Manual" button. Cook on HIGH 15 minutes.
6. When done, naturally release pressure. Remove the lid.
7. Remove loaf pan. Allow to rest 5 minutes before slicing. Serve.

Nutrition information per serving:

- Calories: 394
- Fat: 25.45g
- Carbohydrates: 1.71g
- Dietary Fiber: 0g
- Protein: 37g

Syrian-Style Shakriyeh - Lamb Yogurt Stew

Time: 1 hour
Servings: 6
Ingredients:

- 2 pounds boneless lamb shoulder, cut into bite-sized pieces
- 8 cups homemade low-sodium chicken broth or water
- 1 large red onion or yellow onion, finely chopped
- 4 Tablespoons of sea salt, divided
- 2 Tablespoons arrowroot powder
- 4 Tablespoons toasted pine nuts (for garnishing)
- 2 cups unsweetened coconut yogurt or goat yogurt

Instructions:

1. Add lamb pieces, chicken broth, and 2 tablespoons of the salt to Instant Pot.
2. Lock, seal the lid. Press "Manual" button. Cook on HIGH 40 minutes.
3. When done, quick release or naturally release pressure. Remove the lid.
4. Remove lamb pieces from Instant Pot.
5. In a blender, combine yogurt, salt, arrowroot powder. Pulse until smooth.
6. Press "Sauté" function. Slowly stir in yogurt mixture with liquid. Simmer until it combines and thickens. Return cooked lamed to pot. Simmer 3 minutes.
7. Transfer lamb and sauce to a serving platter. Garnish with toasted pine nuts. Serve.

Nutrition information per serving:

- Calories: 459
- Fat: 17g
- Carbohydrates: 17g
- Dietary Fiber: 1g
- Protein: 53g

Chipotle Braised Lamb

Time: 48 minutes
Servings: 4
Ingredients:

- 4 lamb shanks
- 2 Tablespoons olive oil
- 1 chipotle in adobo sauce
- 1 cup homemade low-sodium chicken broth
- 2 garlic cloves, minced, 1 medium red onion, thinly sliced
- 1 x 15-ouunce can pureed pumpkin
- 4 carrots, peeled, diced, 1 medium beet
- 1 Tablespoon sea salt, 1 Tablespoon garlic powder, 1 Tablespoon organic ground cumin, 1 Tablespoon onion powder, 1 teaspoon organic ground coriander
- 1 teaspoon organic mustard seasoning, 1 teaspoon pepper

Instructions:

1. In a small bowl, add all the seasonings and spices. Mix until well incorporated.
2. Sprinkle the seasoning mixture over the lamb shanks.
3. Press the "Sauté" function on your Instant Pot and add the olive oil.
4. Once hot, working in batches, sear the lamb shanks for 5 minutes per side or until brown. Remove and set aside. Turn off "Sauté" setting.
5. In a blender or food processor, add the chipotle, beet, pureed pumpkin, and chicken broth. Blend until smooth.
6. Add sliced onions, minced garlic, and chipotle mixture to your Instant Pot. Place the lamb shanks on top.
7. Lock, seal the lid. Press "Manual" button. Cook on HIGH 45 minutes.
8. When done, naturally release pressure 15 minutes, then quick release remaining pressure. Remove the lid.
9. Transfer lamb to a serving platter.
10. Press "Sauté" function on Instant Pot. Simmer until thickened, stirring occasionally. Return lamb to pot. Stir until coated. Serve.

Nutrition information per serving:

- Calories: 743
- Fat: 31.3g
- Carbohydrates: 18.2g
- Dietary Fiber: 5.3g
- Protein: 94.1g

Lamb Meatballs

Time: 16 minutes
Servings: 6
Ingredients:

- 2 pounds extra lean grass-fed ground lamb
- 2 Tablespoons olive oil
- 2 large eggs
- 4 garlic cloves, minced
- 6 medium shallots, peeled, finely chopped
- 1 teaspoon organic ground cinnamon powder
- ½ cup dry white wine
- 1 cup homemade low-sodium chicken broth
- 2 Tablespoons unsweetened coconut cream or organic heavy cream
- 2 Tablespoons coconut flour or almond flour
- ¼ cup fresh rosemary, finely chopped
- ¼ cup fresh parsley, finely chopped
- 1 Tablespoon Cajun seasoning
- 2 teaspoons sea salt
- 1 teaspoon black pepper

Instructions:

1. In a large bowl, combine ground lamb, egg, garlic, shallots, cinnamon powder, coconut flour, cream, rosemary, parsley, Cajun seasoning, salt, pepper. Mix well.
2. Form meatballs. Set aside.
3. Press "Sauté" function on Instant Pot. Add the olive oil.
4. Once hot, working in batches, add the lamb meatballs and cook until browned. Turn off "Sauté" function.
5. Return meatballs to Instant Pot. Pour in wine and chicken broth. Close, seal the lid. Press "Manual" button. Cook on HIGH 8 minutes.
6. When done, quick release pressure. Remove the lid.
7. Stir. Transfer the meatballs to a platter. Serve.

Nutrition information per serving:

- Calories: 437
- Fat: 19g
- Carbohydrates: 14g
- Dietary Fiber: 2g
- Protein: 47g

Lamb Stew

Time: 29 minutes
Servings: 4
Ingredients:

- 1 pound lamb stewing meat, cut into bite-sized pieces
- 1 pound fresh asparagus, trimmed and cut into 1-inch pieces
- ¼ cup tahini sauce
- Juice and zest from 1 medium lemon
- 1 medium yellow onion, finely chopped
- 6 garlic cloves, minced
- 1 cup homemade low-sodium chicken broth
- 2 Tablespoons ghee or non-dairy butter
- ½ cup fresh parsley, finely chopped
- ½ cup fresh mint, finely chopped
- 2 teaspoons salt
- 1 teaspoon pepper

Instructions:

1. Add the ghee or non-dairy butter, lamb stew meat, finely chopped yellow onion, minced garlic, chicken broth, salt, and black pepper to your Instant Pot.
2. Lock, seal the lid. Press "Manual" button. Cook on HIGH 16 minutes.
3. When done, naturally release pressure. Remove the lid.
4. Stir in asparagus pieces, tahini sauce, lemon juice and zest, parsley, mint. Allow to heat 5 minutes. Transfer to serving platter. Serve.

Nutrition information per serving:

- Calories: 387
- Fat: 22.9g
- Carbohydrates: 9.1g
- Dietary Fiber: 3.9g
- Protein: 37.2g

Leg of Lamb with Mushroom Gravy

Time: 2 hours
Servings: 8
Ingredients:

- 4 pounds boneless leg of lamb
- 2 Tablespoons olive oil or coconut oil
- 4 cups of water
- 2 cups mushrooms
- 2 Tablespoons arrowroot powder
- 3 Tablespoons non-dairy butter or ghee
- ½ cup white wine
- 1 Tablespoon dried thyme
- 1 Tablespoon dried oregano
- 1 Tablespoon garlic powder
- 1 Tablespoon onion powder
- 1 Tablespoon fresh parsley
- Pinch of salt, pepper

Instructions:

1. In a bowl, combine the thyme, oregano, garlic powder, onion powder, parsley, salt, and black pepper. Season the leg of lamb with the spice mix.
2. Press "Sauté" function on Instant Pot. Add the olive oil
3. Once hot, sear the leg of lamb on all sides. Remove and set aside.
4. Deglaze your Instant Pot with the white wine. Simmer until reduced by half and scrape up any browned bits. Turn off "Sauté" function on Instant Pot.
5. Add mushrooms and water to Instant Pot. Return leg of lamb to pot.
6. Lock, seal the lid and ensure the valve is closed. Press the "Manual" button and cook for 90 minutes on High Pressure.
7. When done, naturally release pressure. Remove the lid. Remove lamb, set aside.
8. Using an immersion blender, blend the mushroom with the liquid until smooth. Stir in arrowroot powder, allow to thicken. Return lamb to pot. Stir to coat.
9. Transfer to platter. Serve.

Nutrition information per serving:

- Calories: 510
- Fat: 25g
- Carbohydrates: 1g
- Dietary Fiber: 0.2g
- Protein: 64g

Lamb Shawarma

Time: 27 minutes
Servings: 8
Ingredients:

- 5 pounds boneless lamb shoulder
- ½ cup coconut oil
- 4 Tablespoons fresh lime juice
- 1 cup of fresh cilantro, finely chopped
- 4 garlic cloves, minced
- 1 3-inch fresh ginger, peeled and finely minced
- Pinch of salt, pepper
- 1 Tablespoon dried sumac seasoning
- 1 Tablespoon nutmeg, finely grated
- 1 Tablespoon cumin seeds
- 1 teaspoon fennel seeds
- 1 Tablespoon regular paprika or smoked paprika
- 2 teaspoons organic ground cinnamon powder

Instructions:

1. In a large Ziploc bag or large mixing bowl, add coconut oil, lime juice, paprika, ground cinnamon, fennel seeds, cumin seeds, fresh cilantro, nutmeg, sumac, pepper, salt, garlic, ginger. Mix well.
2. Place lamb shoulder in Ziploc or covered bowl and marinate in fridge overnight.
3. When ready to cook, add lamb and marinade to Instant Pot.
4. Lock, seal the lid. Press "Manual" button. Cook on HIGH 9 minutes.
5. When done, naturally release pressure 15 minutes, then quick release remaining pressure. Remove the lid.
6. Transfer lamb to a platter. Wait 10 minutes before carving. Serve.

Nutrition information per serving:

- Calories: 983
- Fat: 72.23g
- Carbohydrates: 3.2g
- Dietary Fiber: 1g
- Protein: 63.1g

Sweet Potato and Lamb Stew

Time: 50 minutes
Servings: 6
Ingredients:

- 2 pounds boneless lamb shoulder, cut into bite-sized pieces
- 2 Tablespoon olive oil
- 1 pound sweet potatoes, peeled, cubed
- 1 medium yellow onion, finely chopped
- 4 garlic cloves, thinly sliced
- 2-inches fresh organic ginger root, peeled and finely chopped
- 1 teaspoon organic cumin powder
- 2 teaspoons organic ground coriander powder
- 1 Tablespoon organic pureed pumpkin
- 1 cup homemade low-sodium chicken broth
- 1 cinnamon stick
- 1 Tablespoon fresh parsley, finely chopped
- Pinch of salt, pepper

Instructions:

1. In a bowl, combine cumin, coriander, salt, pepper. Season lamb with spice mix.
2. Press "Sauté" function on Instant Pot. Add the olive oil.
3. Once hot, working in batches if necessary, add lamb pieces, cook until brown. Remove and set aside.
4. Add onions to Instant Pot. Cook 4 minutes. Add garlic to pot. Cook 2 minutes. Add the ginger, and pureed pumpkin. Sauté for 1 minute, stirring consistently.
5. Add the cinnamon stick and chicken broth to your Instant Pot.
6. Close, seal the lid. Press "Manual" button. Cook on HIGH 25 minutes.
7. When done, naturally release pressure. Remove the lid.
8. Add sweet potatoes to pot. Close, seal the lid. Cook on HIGH 10 minutes.
9. When done, quick release pressure. Remove the lid. Remove cinnamon stick.
10. Transfer to bowls. Garnish with fresh parsley. Serve.

Nutrition information per serving:

- Calories: 410
- Fat: 16g
- Carbohydrates: 21g
- Dietary Fiber: 4g
- Protein: 43g

Lamb Rogan

Time: 15 minutes
Servings: 4
Ingredients:

- 1 pound lamb stewing meat, cut into 2-inch pieces
- ¼ cup unsweetened coconut milk yogurt
- 1½ teaspoons organic garam masala
- 1 Tablespoon coconut oil
- 2 bay leaves
- 3 green cardamom pods, opened
- 1 teaspoon of ground cinnamon powder
- 2 garlic cloves, minced
- 1 teaspoon organic ground cumin, 1 teaspoon organic ground ginger
- 1 cup pureed pumpkin
- ½ teaspoon organic chili powder, 1 Tablespoon fresh coriander, finely chopped
- 1 teaspoon salt, 1 teaspoon cumin seeds, 1 teaspoon fennel seeds,

Instructions

1. In a bowl, add lamb stewing meat, coconut milk yogurt, garam masala. Stir until coated. Place in refrigerator. Marinate overnight.
2. Press "Sauté" function on Instant Pot. Add the coconut oil.
3. Once hot, add the garlic. Cook 2 minutes. Add lamb pieces. Sear all sides.
4. Lock, seal the lid. Press "Manual" button. Cook on HIGH 9 minutes.
5. When done, quick release pressure. Remove the lid. Remove bay leaves.
6. Press "Sauté" function. Simmer until liquid reduced/ reaches desired consistency. Season as needed. Transfer to bowls. Garnish with fresh coriander. Serve.

Nutrition information per serving:

- Calories: 199
- Fat: 6.9g
- Carbohydrates: 8g
- Dietary Fiber: 3g
- Protein: 18g

Hong-Kong Lamb

Time: 30 minutes
Servings: 6
Ingredients:

- 2½ pounds boneless lamb breasts, cut into bite-sized pieces
- 3 Tablespoons olive oil and coconut oil
- 13 thin slices fresh peeled ginger
- 6 scallions, chopped
- 3 Tablespoons Shaoxing wine
- 3 Tablespoons low-sodium coconut aminos
- 2 Tablespoons oyster sauce
- 6 large dried Shiitake mushrooms
- ¼ cup of Zhu Hou sauce
- 1 organic bamboo shoot, peeled, thinly sliced
- 4 small carrots, diced, 1 cup celery, diced, 1 cup shredded bok choy
- Pinch of salt, pepper
- 4 cups homemade low-sodium chicken broth or water

Instructions:

1. Soak shiitake mushrooms in water 30 minutes. Once soaked, remove, reserve the water. Cut mushrooms in half.
2. Press "Sauté" function on Instant Pot. Add 2 tablespoons of oil to pot.
3. Once hot, working in batches, add lamb pieces, sear all sides. Set aside.
4. Add remaining oil to pot. Once hot, add ginger, and scallions. Sauté 3 minutes.
5. Return lamb to pot, along with remaining ingredients.
6. Close, seal the lid. Press "Manual" button. Cook on HIGH 15 minutes.
7. When done, allow full natural release. Remove the lid. Stir the ingredients. Season as needed. Ladle into bowls. Garnish with fresh parsley. Serve.

Nutrition information per serving:

- Calories: 457
- Fat: 21.2g
- Carbohydrates: 8.2g
- Dietary Fiber: 2g
- Protein: 54.7g

Vegan and Vegetable Recipes

Cauliflower Tikka Masala

Time: 10 minutes
Servings: 4
Ingredients:

- 1 large cauliflower head, chopped into florets
- ½ cup unsweetened coconut cream or unsweetened non-dairy yogurt
- 1 medium beet, peeled, peeled, diced
- ½ cup pumpkin puree
- ½ cup organic low-sodium bone broth
- 2 Tablespoons ghee or non-dairy butter
- 1 medium red onion, finely chopped, 4 garlic cloves, minced
- 1 1-inch fresh ginger, peeled, grated, 1 Tablespoon dried fenugreek leaves
- 1 Tablespoon fresh parsley, finely chopped
- 1 Tablespoon garam masala
- 1 teaspoon smoked or regular paprika
- 1 teaspoon organic ground turmeric
- 1 teaspoon organic chili powder
- Garnish: roasted cashews, finely chopped cilantro

Instructions:

1. Press "Sauté" function on Instant Pot. Add the ghee.
2. Once melted, add onion. Cook 3 minutes. Add garlic, grated ginger. Cook 2 minutes more. Add fenugreek, paprika, chili powder, turmeric, garam masala, and parsley. Cook 1 minute, stirring frequently.
3. In a blender, combine the beet, pumpkin puree, and bone broth. Blend until slightly chunky. Add to ingredients in the Instant Pot. Stir in the cauliflower.
4. Lock, seal the lid. Press "Manual" button. Cook on HIGH 2 minutes.
5. When done, allow to sit for 1 minute before quick releasing pressure. Remove lid.
6. Stir in cream until well combined. Ladle in bowls. Garnish with roasted cashews, cilantro. Serve.

Nutrition information per serving:

- Calories: 243
- Fat: 8.3g
- Carbohydrates: 33.23g
- Dietary Fiber: 11.96g
- Protein: 13.4g

Barbecue Jackfruit

Time: 16 minutes
Servings: 6
Ingredients:

- 2 x 20-ounce cans jackfruit, drained, chopped
- 1 cup homemade low-sodium vegetable broth
- 1 cup ghee or non-dairy butter, melted
- ½ cup vinegar
- Juice from 1 fresh lemon
- 1 Tablespoon Worcestershire sauce
- 2 teaspoons paprika
- 1 teaspoon onion powder
- 1 teaspoon garlic powder
- 2 teaspoons salt
- 1 teaspoon pepper
- Lettuce leaves for serving

Instructions:

1. Add jackfruit and vegetable broth to Instant Pot.
2. Lock, seal the lid. Press "Manual" button. Cook on HIGH 5 minutes.
3. When done, naturally release pressure. Remove the lid.
4. Using a colander, drain liquid from jackfruit. Return fruit to Instant Pot. Using a potato masher, smash the fruit slightly.
5. In a bowl, combine melted ghee, vinegar, lemon juice, Worcestershire sauce, paprika, garlic powder, onion powder, salt, and black pepper. Stir well. Pour mixture over the jackfruit.
6. Press "Sauté" function. Warm for 5 minutes. Ladle over lettuce leaves. Serve.

Nutrition information per serving:

- Calories: 488
- Fat: 34.8g
- Carbohydrates: 45.7g
- Dietary Fiber: 3g
- Protein: 3.7g

Sweet Potato Hummus

Time: 23 minutes
Servings: 4
Ingredients:

- ½ pound sweet potatoes, peeled, chopped
- 1½ cups homemade low-sodium vegetable broth
- ⅓ cup organic tahini sauce
- ¼ cup freshly squeezed lemon juice
- 2 Tablespoons coconut oil
- 2 garlic cloves, minced
- Pinch of salt, pepper

Instructions:

1. Add potatoes, vegetable broth to Instant Pot.
2. Close, seal the lid. Press "Manual" button. Cook on HIGH 20 minutes.
3. When done, naturally release pressure. Remove lid. Transfer potatoes to a bowl.
4. Transfer sweet potatoes to a food processor with ½ cup of liquid from Instant Pot.
5. Add tahini sauce, lemon juice, coconut oil, garlic cloves, salt, pepper to potatoes.
6. Blend until mixture is smooth and creamy. Stir. Add seasoning as needed.
7. Transfer mixture to covered bowl, or glass jar. Refrigerate until ready to serve.

Nutrition information per serving:

- Calories: 249
- Fat: 17.3g
- Carbohydrates: 20.4g
- Dietary Fiber: 4.3g
- Protein: 4.4g

Cauliflower Risotto

Time: 10 minutes
Servings: 4
Ingredients:

- 12 asparagus, remove woodsy stem, diced
- 1 cup organic fresh broccoli florets, 1 cup organic baby carrots
- 1 cup fresh leeks, finely chopped, 2 garlic cloves, minced
- 1 cup fresh baby spinach, ½ bunch chives, thinly sliced
- 1 medium yellow onion, finely chopped
- 1½ cups cauliflower rice
- 4 cups homemade low-sodium vegetable broth
- 2 Tablespoons olive oil
- 1 teaspoon fresh thyme, ½ teaspoon garlic powder, ¼ teaspoon red pepper flakes
- 1 teaspoon fresh lemon zest, 2 Tablespoons fresh lemon juice
- ¼ cup ghee or non-dairy butter
- Pinch of salt, pepper

Instructions:

1. Line a baking sheet with parchment paper. Place asparagus, broccoli, and carrots in a single layer on the tray. Drizzle olive oil. Season with salt and pepper.
2. Place baking sheet in 400°F oven 15 minutes, until broccoli is tender. Remove, set aside. Once cooled, dice in small pieces.
3. Press "Sauté" function on Instant Pot. Add 1 tablespoon of olive oil.
4. Once hot, add onion. Cook 4 minutes. Add garlic, leeks. Cook 2 minutes. Add cauliflower rice. Sauté 1 minute.
5. Stir in vegetable broth, ghee or non-dairy butter, and fresh thyme.
6. Lock, seal the lid. Press "Manual" button. Cook on HIGH 7 minutes.
7. When done, quick release pressure. Remove the lid.
8. Press "Sauté" function. Stir in asparagus, broccoli, carrots, leeks, spinach, garlic powder, red pepper flakes, lemon zest, and lemon juice. Sauté 1 minute, until spinach wilts. Ladle in bowls. Garnish with chives. Serve.

Nutrition information per serving:

- Calories: 278
- Fat: 21.5g
- Carbohydrates: 15.3g
- Dietary Fiber: 4.3g
- Protein: 8.4g

Mexican-Inspired Posole

Time: 50 minutes
Servings: 8
Ingredients:

- 1 large head cauliflower, finely chopped
- 1 medium yellow onion, finely chopped
- 8 garlic cloves, minced
- 2 x 20-ounce cans jackfruit
- ½ cup coconut oil or olive oil
- ½ cup New Mexico red chile powder
- 1 teaspoon organic ground cumin powder
- 1 teaspoon organic Mexican dried oregano
- ¾ cup coconut flour or almond flour
- 6 cups homemade low-sodium vegetable broth
- Pinch of salt, pepper

Instructions:

1. Press "Sauté" function on Instant Pot. Add coconut oil.
2. Once hot, add onion. Cook 4 minutes. Add garlic. Cook 1 minute.
3. Stir in coconut flour, red chile powder, cumin, oregano, salt, pepper. Cook 3 minutes. Stir in 2 cups of the vegetable broth, jackfruit, and cauliflower florets.
4. Break the jackfruit and cauliflower florets apart using a potato masher. Stir in remaining vegetable broth.
5. Close, seal the lid. Press "Manual" button. Cook on HIGH 10 minutes.
6. When done, naturally release pressure. Remove the lid. Stir ingredients.
7. Ladle into bowls. Serve.

Nutrition information per serving:

- Calories: 314
- Fat: 17.4g
- Carbohydrates: 39.3g
- Dietary Fiber: 3.7g
- Protein: 7.3g

Mushroom Stir-Fry

Time: 33 minutes   Servings: 2
Ingredients:

- 4 cups mushrooms, finely sliced
- 2 Tablespoons of olive oil
- 1 teaspoon of cumin seeds
- 1 strand curry leaves

- 3 Tablespoons homemade low-sodium vegetable broth
- ½ teaspoon mustard seeds
- ¼ teaspoon turmeric powder
- Pinch of salt, pepper

Instructions:

1. Press "Sauté" function on Instant Pot. Add the olive oil.
2. Once hot, add cumin seeds, mustard seeds, curry leaves, turmeric, salt, pepper. Stir. Add the mushrooms and vegetable broth. Turn off "Sauté" function.
3. Close, seal the lid. Press "Steam" function. Cook on HIGH 2 minutes.
4. When done, quick release pressure. Remove the lid.
5. Press "Sauté" function. Simmer until all liquid has evaporated.
6. Ladle in bowls. Garnish with fresh parsley. Serve.

Nutrition information per serving:

- Calories: 150
- Fat: 14.4g

- Carbohydrates: 4.7g

- Dietary Fiber: 1.4g
- Protein: 4.4g

Garlic Green Beans

Servings: 4

Time: 8 minutes
Ingredients:

- 1 pound fresh green beans, trimmed, chopped
- 6 garlic cloves, minced
- ¼ cup ghee, melted

- ½ cup homemade low-sodium vegetable broth
- Juice from ½ medium fresh lemon
- Pinch of salt, pepper

Instructions:

1. Press "Sauté" function on Instant Pot. Add the ghee.
2. Once melted, add garlic. Cook 1 minute, stirring occasionally.
3. Add green beans. Stir. Pour in vegetable broth.
4. Close, seal the lid. Press "Manual" button. Cook on HIGH 5 minutes.
5. When done, quick release pressure. Remove the lid.
6. Squeeze fresh lemon juice over the green beans. Season with salt and pepper.
7. Transfer to a platter. Serve.

Nutrition information per serving:

- Calories: 177
- Fat: 12.8g

- Carbohydrates: 14g
- Dietary Fiber: 2g

- Protein: 3.8g

Sweet Potato Curry - Aloo Saag

Time: 30 minutes
Servings: 4
Ingredients:

- 1 medium red onion, finely chopped
- 4 garlic cloves, minced
- ½ teaspoon organic cumin seeds
- 2 Tablespoons coconut oil, melted
- ½-inch fresh ginger, peeled, grated
- 1 cup fresh baby spinach
- 2 medium sweet potatoes, peeled, cubed
- 1 cup cauliflower florets, chopped
- Pinch of salt, pepper, ½ teaspoon turmeric powder
- ½ teaspoon garam masala powder, ½ teaspoon ground cumin powder
- Juice from 1 lime
- 2 cups homemade low-sodium vegetable broth

Instructions:

1. In a blender/or food processor, add spinach, ginger, vegetable broth. Blend until smooth. Set aside.
2. Press "Sauté" function on Instant Pot. Add the coconut oil.
3. Once hot, add onion. Cook 4 minutes. Add garlic. Cook 2 minutes.
4. Stir in remaining ingredients, including pureed spinach.
5. Lock, seal the lid. Press "Manual" button. Cook on HIGH 4 minutes.
6. When done, quick release pressure. Remove the lid.
7. Stir ingredients. Season as needed. Ladle in bowls. Serve.

Nutrition information per serving:

- Calories: 110
- Fat: 5.3g
- Carbohydrates: 14.9g
- Dietary Fiber: 4.2g
- Protein: 5.1g

Mashed Cauliflower with Spinach

Time: 15 minutes
Servings: 4
Ingredients:

- 1 large head of cauliflower, cut into florets
- 1 Tablespoon flavorless oil
- 1 small yellow onion, finely chopped
- 2 cups organic baby spinach
- 2 garlic cloves, minced
- 2 Tablespoons ghee or non-dairy butter
- ½ cup unsweetened coconut cream or organic heavy cream
- Pinch of salt, pepper
- 1 cup homemade vegetable broth
- 6 sprigs fresh thyme

Instructions:

1. Press "Sauté" function on Instant Pot. Add the oil.
2. Add onion. Cook 4 minutes. Add garlic. Cook 2 minutes. Stir in thyme.
3. Add 1 cup of water, and trivet to Instant Pot. Place cauliflower on top.
4. Lock, seal the lid. Press "Manual" button. Cook on HIGH 15 minutes.
5. When done, naturally release pressure 10 minutes, then quick release remaining pressure. Remove the lid.
6. Remove trivet. Discard liquid. Return cauliflower to pot.
7. While pot is still hot, add ghee, spinach, salt, black pepper, and cream. Using potato masher, mash ingredients until combined. Season. Transfer to bowl. Serve.

Nutrition information per serving:

- Calories: 111
- Fat: 4.3g
- Carbohydrates: 9.8g
- Dietary Fiber: 4.1g
- Protein: 9.83g

Sweet Potato, Cauliflower, Broccoli Stir-Fry

Time: 10 minutes
Servings: 6
Ingredients:

- 4 cups cauliflower florets
- 4 cups broccoli florets
- 2 medium sweet potatoes, peeled, cubed
- 4 Tablespoons ghee or non-dairy butter
- 1 medium yellow onion, finely chopped
- 4 garlic cloves, minced
- 1 Tablespoon fresh parsley, finely chopped
- Pinch of salt, pepper
- ⅛ cup of water
- Sesame seeds for serving

Instructions:

1. Press "Sauté" function on Instant Pot. Add the ghee.
2. Once hot, add onion. Cook 4 minutes. Add garlic. Cook 2 minutes.
3. Add sweet potatoes. Cook 3 minutes, stirring occasionally.
4. Add broccoli, cauliflower to pot. Add water.
5. Lock, seal the lid. Press "Manual" button. Cook on HIGH 2 minutes.
6. When done, quick release pressure. Remove the lid. Stir in parsley, salt, pepper.
7. Transfer to platter. Garnish with sesame seeds. Serve.

Nutrition information per serving:

- Calories: 193
- Fat: 8g
- Carbohydrates: 21g
- Dietary Fiber: 5g
- Protein: 4.83g

Appetizer and Side Dish Recipes

Cinnamon Baby Carrots

Servings: 8

Time: 8 minutes
Ingredients:

- 2 pounds fresh organic baby carrots
- ½ cup water
- 2 Tablespoons ghee or non-dairy butter, melted
- 2 teaspoons organic ground cinnamon powder
- ½ teaspoon organic pure vanilla extract
- 1 teaspoon salt

Instructions:

1. Add the water, and a steamer basket to Instant Pot.
2. Place carrots in steamer basket. Season with salt.
3. Close, seal the lid. Press "Manual" button. Cook on HIGH 2 minutes.
4. When done, quick release pressure. Remove the lid.
5. Remove steamer basket. Discard water. Return carrots to Instant Pot.
6. While pot is still hot, stir in melted ghee, vanilla extract, cinnamon powder.
7. Transfer to a platter. Serve.

Nutrition information per serving:

- Calories: 73
- Fat: 2.9g
- Carbohydrates: 11.2g
- Dietary Fiber: 2.8g
- Protein: 1g

Southern-Style Cabbage

Time: 9 minutes
Ingredients:

Servings: 8

- 1 large head of fresh green cabbage, cored, chopped
- 8 to 12 slices bacon, chopped
- ¼ cup ghee or non-dairy butter
- 2 cups homemade low-sodium chicken broth
- Pinch of salt, pepper

Instructions:

1. Press "Sauté" function on Instant Pot. Cook the bacon until brown.
2. Add ghee or non-dairy butter, allow to melt.
3. Stir in cabbage, chicken broth, salt, black pepper.
4. Close, seal the lid. Press "Manual" button. Cook on HIGH 3 minutes.
5. When done, quick release pressure. Remove the lid.
6. Transfer cabbage to serving platter. Allow to cool slightly. Serve.

Nutrition information per serving:

- Fat: 18.5g
- Carbohydrates: 9.5g
- Protein: 12.6g

Ginger Carrots

Time: 10 minutes   Servings: 10

Ingredients:

- 2 pounds fresh organic baby carrots
- 1 cup fresh orange juice
- 1 Tablespoon freshly squeezed lemon juice
- 4 Tablespoons ghee or non-dairy butter, melted
- 1 teaspoon organic ground ginger
- 1 teaspoon organic ground cinnamon
- 1 teaspoon sea salt

Instructions:

1. Add listed ingredients to Instant Pot. Stir well.
2. Close, seal the lid. Press "Manual" button. Cook on HIGH 3 minutes.
3. When done, quick release pressure. Remove the lid.
4. Transfer carrots to serving dish.
5. Press "Sauté" function on Instant Pot. Simmer until sauce thickens.
6. Ladle sauce over the carrots. Serve.

Nutrition information per serving:

- Calories: 95
- Fat: 5.2g
- Carbohydrates: 11.5g
- Dietary Fiber: 2.3g
- Protein: 0.9g

Balsamic Brussel Sprouts

Time: 23 minutes   Servings: 4

Ingredients:

- 2 cups water
- 1 pound fresh organic brussel sprouts, trimmed, halved
- 6 slices of bacon, chopped
- 4 Tablespoons fresh chives, finely chopped
- 2 Tablespoons balsamic vinegar
- Pinch of salt, pepper

Instructions:

1. Add water, and steamer basket to Instant Pot.
2. Place brussel sprouts on top of steamer basket.
3. Close, seal the lid. Press "Manual" button. Cook on HIGH 2 minutes.
4. When done, quick release pressure. Remove the lid.
5. Transfer brussel sprouts to a bowl. Remove steamer basket, discard the water.
6. Press "Sauté" function. Add chopped bacon. Cook until brown.
7. While pot is still hot, return brussel sprouts to pot with bacon. Stir in balsamic vinegar, salt, pepper. Transfer to platter. Garnish with fresh chives. Serve.

Nutrition information per serving:

- Calories: 206
- Fat: 12.3g
- Carbohydrates: 10.9g
- Dietary Fiber: 4.3g
- Protein: 14.5g

Steamed Asparagus

Time: 5 minutes
Servings: 4
Ingredients:

- 1 pound fresh asparagus, washed, woodsy end cut off
- 1 cup of water
- Pinch of salt, pepper

Instructions:

1. Add the water, and steamer rack to Instant Pot.
2. Place asparagus in a bowl. Drizzle over light layer of oil. Season with salt, pepper
3. Place asparagus on steamer rack.
4. Close, seal the lid. Press "Manual" button. Cook on HIGH 2 minutes.
5. When done, quick release or naturally release pressure. Remove the lid.
6. Remove steamer rack from pot. Transfer asparagus to platter. Serve.

Nutrition information per serving:

- Calories: 23
- Fat: 0.1g
- Carbohydrates: 4.4g
- Dietary Fiber: 2.4g
- Protein: 2.5g

Lemon Bok Choy

Time: 13 minutes
Servings: 4
Ingredients:

- 1 pound baby bok choy, trimmed, sliced in half
- 2 Tablespoons olive oil
- 4 garlic cloves, minced
- 1 teaspoon freshly grated ginger
- 2 Tablespoons low-sodium coconut aminos
- 1 Tablespoon sesame oil
- Juice, zest from 1 medium lemon
- Pinch crushed red pepper flakes
- Pinch of sea salt, pepper

Instructions:

1. Press "Sauté" function on Instant Pot. Add the olive oil.
2. Once hot, add garlic and ginger. Cook 2 minutes.
3. Stir in coconut aminos, lemon juice, lemon zest, and sesame oil.
4. Add bok choy. Stir until coated. Cook 4 minutes, until bok choy wilted.
5. Season with salt, pepper, red pepper flakes. Transfer to platter. Serve.

Nutrition information per serving:

- Calories: 76
- Fat: 7.93g
- Carbohydrates: 2.3g
- Dietary Fiber: 0.3g
- Protein: 1.82g

Asian Bok Choy

Time: 16 minutes
Servings: 6
Ingredients:

- 1 pound baby bok choy, trimmed
- 2 Tablespoons olive oil
- 2 garlic cloves, minced
- 1 teaspoon sesame oil
- 1-inch fresh ginger, peeled and minced
- 1 Tablespoon Chinese seasoned rice vinegar
- 1 Tablespoon low-sodium coconut aminos
- 1 cup homemade low-sodium vegetable broth
- Pinch of salt, pepper

Instructions:

1. Press "Sauté" function on Instant Pot. Add the olive oil.
2. Once hot, Sauté the ginger and garlic cloves for 2 minutes.
3. Add baby bok choy. Cook until slightly wilted.
4. Stir in vegetable broth.
5. Close, seal the lid. Press "Manual" button. Cook on HIGH 5 minutes.
6. When done, quick release pressure. Remove the lid.
7. Drizzle in sesame oil, coconut aminos, and Chinese rice vinegar. Season with salt, pepper.
8. Transfer to bowl. Serve.

Nutrition information per serving:

- Calories: 68
- Fat: 4.86g
- Carbohydrates: 1.84g
- Dietary Fiber: 0.2g
- Protein: 2.06g

Cauliflower and Sweet Potato Salad

Time: 15 minutes
Servings: 8
Ingredients:

- 1½ pounds sweet potatoes, peeled, cubed
- ½ pound cauliflower florets, chopped
- 2 large eggs
- 6 slices of bacon, chopped
- ½ cup homemade Lectin-free mayonnaise
- 1 Tablespoon organic Dijon mustard
- 3 green onions, diced
- 1 Tablespoon fresh parsley, chopped
- Pinch of salt, pepper
- 1 cup of water

Instructions:

1. Add 1 cup of water, and steamer basket to Instant Pot.
2. Place cubed sweet potatoes, 2 large eggs, cauliflower on steamer basket.
3. Close, seal the lid. Press "Manual" button. Cook on HIGH 4 minutes.
4. When done, quick release pressure. Remove the lid.
5. Transfer potatoes and cauliflower to a large bowl. Peel, dice the eggs. Place ingredients in fridge to cool down.
6. Remove steamer rack, and discard water from pot.
7. Press "Sauté" function. Cook the bacon until brown. Turn off pot. Transfer bacon to fridge with other ingredients. Thirty minutes to cool down.
8. Return potatoes, cauliflower, bacon, diced egg to a large bowl. Stir in homemade mayonnaise, Dijon mustard, green onions, parsley, salt, black pepper. Serve.

Nutrition information per serving:

- Calories: 259
- Fat: 12.2g
- Carbohydrates: 29.1g
- Dietary Fiber: 4.3g
- Protein: 8.6g

Lemon and Garlic Broccoli

Time: 23 minutes   Servings: 4

Ingredients:

- 6 cups fresh broccoli florets
- 1 cup of water
- 1 large garlic head
- 2 Tablespoons fresh lemon juice
- 2 Tablespoons + 1 teaspoon of melted coconut oil
- Pinch of crushed red pepper flakes
- Pinch of salt, pepper

Instructions:

1. Add 1 cup of water, and steamer rack to Instant Pot.
2. Place garlic head in skin on steamer rack. Drizzle over melted coconut oil.
3. Close, seal the lid. Press "Manual" button. Cook on HIGH 7 minutes.
4. When done, naturally release pressure 10 minutes, then quick release remaining pressure. Remove the lid.
5. Remove garlic from rack. Squeeze skin from garlic. Place broccoli on steamer rack.
6. Close, seal the lid. Press "Manual" button. Cook on HIGH 10 minutes.
7. When done, quick release pressure. Remove the lid.
8. In a blender, combine cooked garlic cloves, lemon juice, 2 tablespoons coconut oil, red pepper flakes, salt, pepper. Blend until smooth. Transfer broccoli to platter.
9. Pour sauce over broccoli. Serve.

Nutrition information per serving:

- Calories: 153
- Fat: 6.3g
- Carbohydrates: 16.3g
- Dietary Fiber: 4.9g
- Protein: 8.3g

Lemon Butter Brussel Sprouts

Time: 14 minutes   Servings: 4

Ingredients:

- 1 pound fresh brussel sprouts, trimmed, halved
- 1 cup of water
- 4 Tablespoons ghee or non-dairy butter, melted
- Juice and zest from 1 medium lemon

Instructions:

1. Add 1 cup of water, and steamer basket to Instant Pot.
2. Place brussel sprouts on top of steamer basket.
3. Close, seal the lid. Press "Manual" button. Cook on HIGH 2 minutes.
4. When done, quick release pressure. Remove the lid.
5. Remove steamer basket and brussel sprouts. Discard the water.
6. Press "Manual" button. Add ghee or non-dairy butter. Once melted, add lemon juice, zest. Return brussel sprouts to pot. Simmer 5 minutes, until fork tender.
7. Transfer to platter. Serve.

Dessert Recipes

Stuffed Peaches

Time: 20 minutes
Servings: 6
Ingredients:

- 6 organic fresh peaches, tops removed, pitted
- ¼ cup organic coconut flour or organic almond flour
- ¼ cup Swerve sweetener
- 2 Tablespoons ghee or coconut oil
  1 teaspoon organic ground cinnamon powder
- ½ teaspoon pure almond extract
- Pinch of salt

Instructions:

1. In a bowl, combine flour, swerve, oil, cinnamon, almond extract, and salt. Stir well.
2. Divide mixture evenly between the peaches.
3. Add 1 cup of water, and steamer basket to Instant Pot.
4. Place stuffed peaches on top of steamer basket.
5. Lock, seal the lid. Press "Manual" button. Cook on HIGH 3 minutes.
6. When done, quick release pressure. Remove the lid.
7. Transfer peaches to platter. Top with non-dairy ice cream. Serve.

Nutrition information per serving:

- Calories: 172
- Fat: 14.21g
- Carbohydrates: 1.76g
- Dietary Fiber: 0.9g
- Protein: 9.11g

Chocolate Avocado Muffin Bites

Time: 15 minutes
Servings: 6
Ingredients:

- 2 large organic eggs
- 1 cup apple juice
- ½ cup coconut oil, melted
- 3 Tablespoons organic cocoa powder
- 1 cup coconut flour
- ½ teaspoon baking powder
- ½ teaspoon baking soda
- 1 teaspoon organic cinnamon powder
- 2 teaspoons organic vanilla extract
- Pinch of salt
- 1 cup ripe avocados, peeled, pit removed, mashed
- ⅓ cup unsweetened dark chocolate chips

Instructions:

1. In a large bowl, combine listed ingredients. Stir well.
2. Grease ramekins or silicone muffin cups with non-stick cooking spray. Divide and fill with the chocolate avocado mixture.
3. Add 1 cup of water, and trivet to Instant Pot.
4. Place ramekins/ muffin cups on top of trivet.
5. Lock, seal the lid. Press "Manual" button. Cook on HIGH 8 minutes.
6. When done, naturally release pressure. Remove the lid.
7. Transfer to wire rack to cool. Serve.

Nutrition information per serving:

- Calories: 272
- Fat: 25g
- Carbohydrates: 10g
- Dietary Fiber: 3g
- Protein: 4g

Raspberry Curd

Time: 8 minutes
Servings: 6
Ingredients:

- 2 cups fresh raspberries
- 1 cup of swerve or erythritol sweetener
- 2 egg yolks
- 2 Tablespoons ghee or coconut oil
- 1 Tablespoon fresh orange juice
- 2 Tablespoons fresh lemon juice
- ½ teaspoon lemon zest
- Pinch of salt

Instructions:

1. Add listed ingredients to Instant Pot, except egg yolks and ghee. Stir well.
2. Lock, seal the lid. Press "Manual" button. Cook on HIGH 1 minute.
3. When done, naturally release pressure 5 minutes, then quick release remaining pressure. Remove the lid.
4. Using an immersion blender, puree raspberry mixture until smooth.
5. Press "Sauté" function. Stir in egg yolks and ghee to raspberry mixture.
6. Transfer raspberry mixture to covered bowl, or glass jar. Refrigerate.
7. Serve over non-dairy ice cream, or yogurt.

Nutrition information per serving:

- Calories: 115
- Fat: 1.8g
- Carbohydrates: 24.5g
- Dietary Fiber: 3.2g
- Protein: 1.63g

Peppermint Cheesecake

Time: 40 minutes + 4 hours of refrigerating time
Servings: 6

- 2 cups organic cream cheese, softened, ¼ cup sour cream
- 2 large organic eggs
- ½ cup swerve or erythritol sweetener
- 1 Tablespoon coconut, Pinch of salt
- 1½ teaspoons pure vanilla extract, ½ teaspoons pure peppermint extract
- Chocolate Ganache:
- 6-ounces unsweetened chocolate chips, melted
- ⅓ cup organic heavy cream, Pinch of salt
- Crust:
- 1 cup almond flour
- 2 Tablespoons swerve or erythritol sweetener
- 2 Tablespoons ghee or goat butter, melted

Instructions:

1. Combine ingredients for crust. Press down in a spring form pan; choose pan suitable for Instant Pot. Place in freezer for 10 minutes.
2. In a large bowl or blender, combine filling ingredients. Stir well.
3. Pour cheesecake filling in spring form pan. Cover with aluminum foil.
4. Add 1 cup of water, and trivet to Instant Pot. Place spring form pan on top.
5. Close, seal the lid. Press "Manual" button. Cook on HIGH 35 minutes.
6. When done, naturally release pressure 15 minutes, then quick release remaining pressure. Remove the lid.
7. Remove pan from pot. Cool on counter 30 minutes, then refrigerate 4 hours.
8. In a bowl, combine chocolate ganache ingredients. Microwave 30 seconds. Stir. Repeat until smooth.
9. Transfer cheesecake to platter. Drizzle over ganache. Serve.

Nutrition information per serving:

- Calories: 453
- Fat: 33.3g
- Carbohydrates: 30g
- Dietary Fiber: 0.8g
- Protein: 9g

Maple Flan

Time: 1 hour and 30 minutes
Servings: 8
Ingredients:

- ½ cup maple syrup
- 3 large organic eggs
- 1½ cups coconut milk
- 1½ cups organic heavy cream
- 1 Tablespoon pure vanilla extract
- ½ teaspoon salt

Instructions:

1. Add half of maple syrup to bottom of Instant Pot soufflé dish.
2. In a bowl, whisk eggs, and quarter cup of maple syrup
3. In a medium saucepan, combine coconut milk, heavy cream, vanilla extract, salt. Simmer on low 5 minutes.
4. Temper hot cream to eggs: Drizzle in small amount of hot cream slowly to beaten eggs. Stir well. Pour in rest of hot cream. Stirring constantly.
5. Using a fine mesh strainer, strain ingredients into soufflé dish. Cover with aluminum foil.
6. Add 3 cups of water, and trivet to Instant Pot. Place soufflé dish on trivet.
7. Lock, seal the lid. Press "Slow Cook" button. Cook on HIGH 75 minutes.
8. When done, quick release pressure. Remove the lid.
9. Transfer soufflé dish to a wire rack. Allow to cool 60 minutes.
10. Refrigerate 4 hours. Serve with non-dairy cream, fresh berries.

Nutrition information per serving:

- Calories: 247
- Fat: 18g
- Carbohydrates: 18.63g
- Dietary Fiber: 1.3g
- Protein: 4.09g

Sweet Potato Chocolate Cake

Time: 1 hour
Servings: 14
Ingredients:

- ½ cup organic coconut flour
- ½ cup organic cocoa powder
- ½ cup chocolate protein powder
- 1 Tablespoon baking powder
- ½ teaspoon baking soda
- 1 cup mashed sweet potato
- ¼ cup swerve or erythritol sweetener
- ½ cup coconut oil, ½ cup of nut butter
- ¾ cup unsweetened coconut milk
- Chocolate Frosting:
- ½ cup coconut oil, melted
- 3 Tablespoons swerve sweetener, ½ cup cocoa powder
- 1 cup unsweetened homemade applesauce
- 1 Tablespoon arrowroot powder

Instructions:

1. In a large bowl, combine coconut flour, cocoa powder, protein powder, baking powder, baking soda. Whisk.
2. In a separate bowl, combine sweet potato, sweetener, coconut oil, nut butter, coconut milk. Stir well.
3. Grease a 7-inch cake pan for Instant Pot with non-stick spray.
4. Pour in batter. Cover with foil.
5. Add 2 cups water, and trivet to Instant Pot. Place cake pan on trivet.
6. Close, seal the lid. Press "Manual" button. Cook on HIGH 40 minutes.
7. When done, naturally release pressure. Remove the lid.
8. In a large bowl, add frosting ingredients. Stir well. Refrigerate 20 minutes.
9. Remove cake from Instant Pot. Allow to cool completely.
10. Spread chocolate frosting over cake. Serve.

Nutrition information per serving:

- Calories: 263
- Fat: 22g
- Carbohydrates: 15g
- Dietary Fiber: 6g
- Protein: 4g

Apple Cake

Time: 1 hour
Servings: 6
Ingredients:

- 2 cups fresh red or green apples, peeled, cored, chopped
- ½ cup homemade applesauce
- 1 teaspoon ground cinnamon powder
- ¼ teaspoon ground nutmeg
- 1½ cups almond flour
- ¼ cup goat butter or ghee, melted
- ¼ cup coconut oil
- 2 large eggs
- ½ cup swerve or erythritol sweetener
- ½ cup almonds, roughly chopped
- ½ teaspoon pure vanilla extract
- Pinch of salt

Instructions:

1. In a large bowl, combine listed ingredients, except the almonds. Stir well.
2. Grease a 7-inch cake pan for Instant Pot with non-stick spray.
3. Pour in batter. Top with almonds. Cover pan with foil.
4. Add 1 cup of water, and trivet to Instant Pot. Place cake pan on trivet.
5. Close, seal the lid. Press "Manual" button. Cook on HIGH 60 minutes.
6. When done, naturally release pressure. Remove the lid.
7. Transfer pan to a wire rack. Allow to cool slightly before slicing. Serve.

Nutrition information per serving:

- Calories: 313
- Fat: 27g
- Carbohydrates: 22g
- Dietary Fiber: 3g
- Protein: 5g

Lavender Crème Brulée

Time: 13 minutes　　　　　　　　　　Servings: 4

Ingredients:

- 8 egg yolk
- 2 cups unsweetened coconut cream
- ⅓ cup swerve sweetener
- 1 teaspoon pure vanilla extract
- 1 Tablespoon dried culinary lavender
- 1½ cups water

Instructions:

1. In a bowl, combine coconut cream, and sweetener. Stir well.
2. Whisk in egg yolks. Stir in vanilla extract and lavender.
3. Grease ramekins with nonstick spray. Divide batter evenly between ramekins.
4. Add water and, trivet to Instant Pot. Place ramekins on trivet.
5. Lock, seal the lid. Pres "Manual" button. Cook on HIGH 9 minutes.
6. When done, naturally release pressure. Remove the lid.
7. Transfer ramekins to cool rack. Allow to cool 1 hour at room temperature. Chill in refrigerator 4 hours. Serve with fresh berries.

Nutrition information per serving:

- Calories: 382
- Fat: 36.3g
- Carbohydrates: 13g
- Dietary Fiber: 2g
- Protein: 4.3g

Almond Butter Chocolate Cake

Time: 8 minutes　　　　　　　　　　Servings: 1

Ingredients:

- 1 Tablespoon almond butter, melted
- 1 teaspoon ghee, melted
- ½ teaspoon pure vanilla extract
- 1 Tablespoon unsweetened coconut cream
- 1 large organic egg
- 2 Tablespoons swerve sweetener
- 2 Tablespoons cocoa powder

Instructions:

1. In a large bowl, combine listed ingredients, except the almond butter. Stir well.
2. Grease a ramekin with non-stick spray. Pour in batter.
3. Pour 1 cup of water, and trivet to Instant Pot. Place ramekin on trivet.
4. Lock, seal the lid. Press "Manual" button. Cook on HIGH 2 minutes.
5. When done, quick release pressure. Remove the lid.
6. Drizzle melted almond butter over ramekin cake. Serve.

Nutrition information per serving:

- Calories: 257
- Fat: 22.6g
- Carbohydrates: 20.1g
- Dietary Fiber: 5.2g
- Protein: 11.2g

Orange Essential Oil Cheesecake

Time: 33 minutes
Servings: 6
Crust Ingredients:

- 1 ½ cup of coconut flour, almond flour or grounded mixed nuts
- 2 Tablespoons of Swerve sweetener or stevia
- 3 Tablespoons of ghee or coconut oil, melted

Orange Cheesecake Filling Ingredients:

- 2 cups of raw cashews
- 1 cup of unsweetened coconut cream
- 1 Tablespoon of arrowroot powder
- 1 Tablespoon of coconut oil, melted
- 1 teaspoon of lime zest
- 4 Tablespoons of freshly squeezed orange juice
- 1 teaspoon of orange essential oil

Instructions:

1. In a bowl, combine crust ingredients. Mix well with your hands, but not long.
2. Press the crust into an Instant Pot spring form pan.
3. Place in a 350°F oven. Bake approximately 10 minutes.
4. In a blender, combine orange cheesecake filling ingredients. Blend until smooth.
5. Pour filling into crusted spring form pan. Cover with foil.
6. Add 2 cups water, and trivet to Instant Pot. Place spring form pan on trivet.
7. Lock, seal the lid. Press "Manual" button. Cook on HIGH 25 minutes.
8. When done, naturally release pressure. Remove the lid.
9. Transfer pan to a cooling rack. Cool 1 hour at room temperature. Chill in refrigerator 4 hours. Top with fresh berries, non-dairy cream. Serve.

Nutrition information per serving:

- Calories: 456
- Fat: 48g
- Carbohydrates: 31g
- Dietary Fiber: 4g
- Protein: 12.3g

Chapter 4: 14-Day Lectin-Free Diet Meal Plan

In this chapter, you will find an efficient Lectin-Free diet meal plan that will last you 2 weeks. This 14-day meal plan will provide you a diverse set of recipes for you to choose from each day. You are free to change the meal plan according to your liking. Enjoy!

Week One

Day One
Meal one: Breakfast Sausage and Cauliflower Mash
Meal two: Lamb Rogan
Meal three: Spinach Sweet Potato Curry - Aloo Saag

Day Two
Meal one: Turkey Sausage Frittata
Meal two: Balsamic Brussel Sprouts
Meal three: Beef Burgundy with Mushrooms

Day Three
Meal one: Cauliflower Pudding
Meal two: Lemon Bok Choy
Meal three: Wine and Coffee Beef Stew

Day Four
Meal one: Spinach and Mushroom Frittata
Meal two: Asian Bok Choy
Meal three: Chipotle Braised Lamb

Day Five
Meal one: Hard Boiled Egg Loaf
Meal two: Cauliflower and Sweet Potato Salad
Meal three: Beef Curry

Day Six
Meal one: Turkey Sausage Frittata
Meal two: Lemon Butter Brussel Sprouts
Meal three: Barbecue Jackfruit

Day Seven
Meal one: Egg Hash
Meal two: Steamed Asparagus
Meal three: Beef Meatballs with Mushroom Sauce

Week Two

Day Eight
Meal one: Egg Frittata with Asparagus
Meal two: Chicken Kale Soup
Meal three: Pork Chops with Red Cabbage

Day Nine
Meal one: Chorizo with Sweet Potato Hash
Meal two: Leek and Cauliflower Soup
Meal three: Lemon Chicken

Day Ten
Meal one: Coconut Yogurt with Berries
Meal two: Chicken Paprikash
Meal three: Sloppy Joes
Day Eleven
Meal one: Spinach and Mushroom Frittata
Meal two: Chicken Lime Avocado Soup
Meal three: Leg of Lamb with Mushroom Gravy
Day Twelve
Meal one: Egg Hash
Meal two: Southern-Style Cabbage
Meal three: Adobo Pork
Day Thirteen
Meal one: Hard Boiled Egg Loaf
Meal two: Chicken Turmeric Soup
Meal three: Lamb Meatballs
Day Fourteen
Meal one: Broccoli and Ham Frittata
Meal two: Hamburger Vegetable Soup
Meal three: Creamy Chicken Thighs

Conclusion

Thank you again for reading my book, "Lectin-Free Instant Pot Cookbook."

Now that you fully read this book, you understand exactly what the Lectin-Free diet is, how you can get started, what to eat, what not to eat, how to follow the diet, and create 100 delicious Lectin-Free recipes using your Instant Pot.

You also have a 14-day Lectin-Free sample meal plan and tips for succeeding in this diet. With this said, I am positive you will experience the many benefits this diet must offer.

Finally, if you enjoyed this book or find something of value from it, I ask you to please take the time to leave an honest review on Amazon. Recommend to your friends and family. This all would be greatly appreciated.

Thank you, and best of luck on your Lectin-Free diet journey!

Appendix: Measuring Units and Conversion

Measuring ingredients is simple and easy unless you are confused on the volume measuring units. To make your culinary experience easier, here is a reference guide to aid in creating the delicious recipes.

Dry Volume Measurements and Conversions

- 1/6 teaspoon = a dash
- 1/8 teaspoon = a pinch
- 3 teaspoons = 1 Tablespoon
- 1/8 cup = 2 Tablespoons
- ¼ cup = 4 Tablespoons
- 1/3 cup = 5 Tablespoons + 1 teaspoon
- ½ cup = 8 Tablespoons
- ¾ cup = 12 Tablespoons
- 1 cup = 16 Tablespoons
- 1 pound= 16 ounces

Liquid Volume Measurements and Conversions

- 8 ounces = 1 cup
- 1 pint = 2 cups
- 1 quart = 2 pints
- 1 gallon = 4 quarts

US to Metric Conversions

- 1/5 teaspoon = 1 ml
- 1 teaspoon = 5 ml
- 1 Tablespoon = 15 ml
- 1 fluid ounce = 30 ml
- 1/5 cup = 50 ml
- 1 cup = 240 ml
- 2 cups =470 ml
- 4 cups =.95 liter
- 4 quarts = 3.8 liters
- 1 ounce = 28 grams
- 1 pound = 454 grams

CPSIA information can be obtained
at www.ICGtesting.com
Printed in the USA
LVHW01s0958161018
593767LV00001B/1/P